PENGUIN CLASSICS

THE CLOUD OF UNKNOWING AND OTHER WORKS

ADVISORY EDITOR: BETTY RADICE

The identity of the author of *The Cloud of Unknowing* is unknown, but he was undoubtedly an English priest who lived during the latter half of the fourteenth century. Six other works are commonly attributed to the same pen; and their words, style, and language suggest those of a country parson from the East Midlands.

•

CLIFTON WOLTERS was born in London, and trained for the priesthood at Durham University and the London College of Divinity. He was Vicar of Wimbledon Park, Rector of Sanderstead, and later Provost of Newcastle. Now retired, he is serving as Chaplain to St Margaret's Convent, East Grinstead. He has also translated Julian of Norwich's *Revelations of Divine Love* and Richard Rolle's *Fire of Love* for the Penguin Classics.

THE CLOUD
OF UNKNOWING

AND OTHER WORKS

TRANSLATED INTO MODERN ENGLISH

WITH AN INTRODUCTION BY

CLIFTON WOLTERS

PENGUIN BOOKS

PENGUIN BOOKS

Published by the Penguin Group
27 Wrights Lane, London w8 5TZ, England
Viking Penguin Inc., 40 West 23rd Street, New York, New York 10010, USA
Penguin Books Australia Ltd, Ringwood, Victoria, Australia
Penguin Books Canada Ltd, 2801 John Street, Markham, Ontario, Canada L3R 1B4
Penguin Books (NZ) Ltd, 182–190 Wairau Road, Auckland 10, New Zealand

Penguin Books Ltd, Registered Offices: Harmondsworth, Middlesex, England

This translation of *The Cloud of Unknowing* first published 1961
Reprinted with *The Epistle of Priory Counsel, Dionysius' Mystical Teaching,*
and *The Epistle of Prayer* 1978
9 10 8

Copyright © Clifton Wolters, 1961, 1978
All rights reserved

Made and printed in Great Britain by
Hazell Watson & Viney Limited
Member of BPCC plc
Aylesbury, Bucks, England
Set in Monotype Bembo

CORONAE MEAE ET GAUDIO
CONJUGI CARISSIMAE
ANIMO GRATISSIMO

CONTENTS

Introduction

The Cloud of Unknowing

The Epistle of Privy Counsel

CONTENTS

INTRODUCTION

THE works translated in this book[1] belong to the devotional classics of the English Church, and are among the greatest of them all. No one who reads them can fail to catch something of their splendour and charm. They spring from an age when English mysticism was in full flower, when Richard Rolle, Walter Hilton, the author of *The Cloud*, and Julian of Norwich,[2] were writing with such timelessness and reality that their influence is as great today as it has ever been since that remarkable inexplicable century.

We are told that the wind of God blows where it lists; certainly the whole of the Western Church was quickened at this time. France, Germany, Flanders, Italy, all bear witness to the same profound stirring. A glance at the names of the outstanding continental mystics confirms it: Mechtild, Gertrude, Angela de Foligno, Eckhart, Tauler, Suso, Catherine of Siena, Ruysbroek, and Thomas à Kempis.[3] It is a noble band and fruitful, and together with the Englishmen, makes a company without parallel in the history of the Church.

The surprising thing about this particular upsurge is that it happened when it did. Western Europe was in the throes of the Hundred Years War; the Black Death was decimating every country it entered; social unrest was showing itself in the English Peasants' Revolt; the Papacy, soon to be split in two, was already 'in captivity' at Avignon; new

1. They are *The Cloud of Unknowing*, *The Epistle of Privy Counsel*, *The Epistle of Prayer*, and *Dionysius' Mystical Teaching*.

2. Their dates are 1300–49; d. 1396; c. 1370; 1343–1413.

3. They died respectively in 1298, 1302, 1309, 1327, 1361, 1365, 1380, 1381, 1471.

ideas were beginning to emerge; heresy was exerting its disintegrating influence; the foredawn of the Renaissance was discernible; and already the premonitory tremors of the cataclysm of the Reformation could be felt. Medieval Christendom was passing away, and modern nationalism was coming to painful birth.

It was in this restless, unsettled age that mysticism revived, and men turned from the rage and storm to consider rather the calm depths that lay beneath. It was as children of their age of course that they 'turned aside to see', and what they saw they describe to us in their own idiom, which reflects the hopes and fears of their day. The fourteenth-century mystic, writing for the first time in the vernacular and with a new emphasis on the individuality of the soul, is a man speaking from the midst of an age of transition. This may well be the reason why these later medievals are treasured by both Anglicans and Romans alike, for both are heirs of the tensions and divisions which stem from those far-off days. We may hope that in this common appreciation and affection they are drawn closer to each other.

Yet for most English-speaking Christians *The Cloud of Unknowing* (the best known of them all) is not even a name, and few of those who have heard of it have gone on to read it or its companion works. There are various reasons for this ignorance, and two of them are obvious: language and subject matter.

Many people find the language a real difficulty. In such editions as are procurable, the Middle English of the original has been little altered, except for a word here and there, and the spelling generally. Thus the pith and vigour of the books can be fully savoured, but their message not so easily understood. They reveal their meaning to those who persevere, and who feel for the archaic, but not many people nowadays seem to have the necessary time or talent. If the Authorized Version of the Bible, published in 1611, is considered difficult to understand and needs modern English versions to explain it, there must be even greater need for a translation of books which were written about 1370.

There is an obvious loss in being deprived of the original language. It has a strength and rhythm and beauty, and a score of memorable phrases, which do not always stand the strain of being translated. Offsetting this, however, is the considerable gain in lucidity, and it is hoped that the translation's inevitable inadequacy will not wholly obscure the freshness and beauty of this fourteenth-century work.

The second reason, the subject matter, is nothing like so baffling once the language has been modernized, and it is to this that the rest of this general introduction and the individual prefaces to each work are devoted. These preliminaries, like the writings themselves, complement each other, and it is possible (in the words of *The Cloud*) that 'peradventure there is some matter therein, in the beginning or in the middle, the which is hanging and not fully declared where it standeth: and if it is not there it is soon after, or else in the end.' But in any case it is the works themselves that count, and the reader's attention is directed to them.

Authorship

The identity of the author of *The Cloud of Unknowing* and its cognates is not known. It is commonly assumed that from the first his intention was to remain anonymous, which with a book of such a title is not altogether inappropriate. There have been countless conjectures, and though some have been ingenious, none has been convincing. The problem may yield ultimately to scholarly probing, but at the moment it is intractable.

Every reader will form his own opinion of the author, and though individual impressions will vary it would commonly be accepted that he was a man convinced of the necessity for God to be at the centre of all life; he had a well-stored and scholarly mind, with a flair for expressing complexities simply; there was more than a streak of the poet in him, and at the same time a saving sense of humour and proportion. Probably most people would feel that they would like to know him, and some at least might wish they could have his guidance today.

The writing of great religious works is not by any means a male preserve – we have only to look at the lists of names in the opening paragraph – but we can safely predicate 'he' of the author of *The Cloud* works, not merely because of the sense of masculinity that pervades the whole, nor because of the knowledge of theology that is revealed, nor even because of the authority with which the young disciple[1] for whom some at least of the books were written is being directed – all these are cumulative, but not conclusive – but because *The Cloud*'s final paragraph reveals him as a priest, dispensing 'God's blessing and mine' (Chapter 75).

About the sphere in which his priesthood was exercised the books say nothing. There is a wide and pleasing diversity of opinion in this matter. He has been variously called 'a secular priest, a cloistered monk, a Carthusian, not a Carthusian, a hermit, a recluse'.[2] If he was not a friar, one of these is almost certainly right. We may guess with Dom Justin McCann[3] that he was a country parson, perhaps in

1. Aged twenty-four. *The Cloud*, Chapter 4.
2. Hodgson, P. *The Cloud of Unknowing*. London, 1958, p. lxxxiii.
3. McCann, Dom J. *The Cloud of Unknowing*. London, 1941, p. xiv.

the East Midlands, with more than a nodding acquaintance of the religious life, and a largish circle of souls under his direction.

A similar uncertainty exists as to their date and place of composition. The most that can be said is that they were written during the latter half of the fourteenth century.[1] *The Cloud* fairly obviously seeks to correct misleading notions based on the works of Richard Rolle, who died in 1349, and in its turn is criticized by another outstanding mystic, Walter Hilton, who died in 1395. Between these two dates it must have been published. With this conclusion the evidence of surviving manuscripts agrees; the earliest comes from the late fourteenth century (or perhaps the very beginning of the fifteenth). All the others are fifteenth century and later.

There are six other works commonly attributed to this same pen, but while they confirm the general conclusions we have indicated, they give no clue to the writer himself. The three most important are included in this volume, namely *The Epistle of Privy Counsel, The Epistle of Prayer*, and *Dionysius' Mystical Teaching*. The others of less general interest are *Benjamin* (a free translation of the book of the same name by Richard of St Victor), *The Epistle of Discretion in the Stirrings of the Soul*, and *The Treatise of the Discerning of Spirits*.

A careful and expert analysis of the words, style, and language points to an East Midland provenance for them all.

No more than this is known. It may be thought disappointing that so much solid research and labour have produced so little result. The value of the books as a whole is unaffected.

1. In the same period Geoffrey Chaucer wrote his *Canterbury Tales* (about 1390).

The Sources

No man writes books like these 'out of the blue'. His mind has been shaped and his outlook fashioned by all sorts of outside influences, some of which he will recall and admit, and others which, because he has assimilated them, he may forget. Yet these last have been just as formative, and very often patient research will discover what they were.

Various and recognizable sources contribute to *The Cloud* series of writings, and in his different works the author acknowledges them. Thus Pseudo-Dionysius and St Augustine are mentioned in *The Cloud* (Chapters 70 and 75), St Bernard in *Privy Counsel* (Chapter 7), Abbot Thomas Gallus (Vercellensis) in the *Mystical Teaching* (Prologue), St Thomas Aquinas in *The Epistle of Prayer*. St Bernard features again in the less important *Discerning of Spirits*, only this time without acknowledgement, for the tract is a reworking and conflation of two of his sermons. Other influences have been suspected. It is thought that the *De Adhaerendo Deo* of Albertus Magnus affected *The Cloud*, and that the hands of Guigo II, Prior of Grande Chartreuse and author of *Scala Claustralium* (d. 1193), and St Gregory, Bishop of Nyssa (*c*. 330–95), and St Gregory, Pope of Rome (*c*. 540–604) are to be detected in the different works.

But the roots of *The Cloud*'s teaching lie not in the authorities just named but in two highly influential writers whose impact on medieval and mystical theology cannot well be measured. The closer to our author in time is Richard of St Victor, and behind much of his thinking (and of *The Cloud* as well) is the sixth-century Dionysius.

Richard was a Scot, but apart from that fact not a great deal is known about him, not even when or where he was born. He was a Canon Regular of the great Abbey of St Victor in Paris, famed for its learning and religion. He became its sub-prior in 1159, and its prior in 1162. He died in 1173, 'still a young man' according to his biographer. He was a voluminous writer on a variety of subjects, and Ottaviano has listed forty-two treatises from his pen. Seemingly the most fruitful period of authorship was from 1153 until his death. Exegete, philosopher, theologian, psychologist, and mystic, his strength lay in the emphasis he placed on the unity of all forms of knowledge. So he set high store on reason, and his approach to contemplation had to be rational. In contemplative ecstasy, however, the use of reason was suspended, but it resumed its function once the experience was ended. His definition of contemplation has been described as 'a power to co-ordinate a variety of perceptions into one all-embracing intuition fixed with wonder on divine things.'[1] His influence was widespread and pervaded much mystical theology in Western Christendom. To the author of *The Cloud* quite clearly Richard's *Benjamin Minor* and *Benjamin Major* were works of predilection, for they have yielded words, paragraphs, and even chapters to *The Cloud of Unknowing*, as well as its distinctive title. Moreover our author made a very successful paraphrase-translation of *Benjamin Minor*, at once more readable and interesting than the Latin original.

The second important source is the so-called Dionysius the Areopagite, or, to give him *The Cloud*'s name, St Denis. Dionysius was the convert of St Paul on his mission to Athens (Acts 17) but the writings ascribed to him cannot possibly be earlier than the beginning of the sixth century, and are believed to have been fathered on him by an unknown Syrian monk. This false ascription of authorship, so distasteful to us today, was a common practice among

1. This comprehensive quotation comes from Clare Kirchberger's *Richard of St Victor: Selected Writings on Contemplation*. London, 1957, p. 30.

the ancients, who sometimes thought they were propagating the teaching of their *noms de plume*, but who, more often, used the name as a means to ensure that their own works would be read and their teaching heeded.

Pseudo-Dionysius' ideas were not new, but his concise little books crystallized and popularized what had hitherto been unformulated, and this and the presumed authority of a New Testament disciple gave his teaching subsequently an influence on Christian mystical theology beyond power to assess. His basic thought is that of the utter incomprehensibility of God.

There are two ways of describing our knowledge of God, and in Western Christendom they have long been called the Positive Way (*via positiva*) and the Negative Way (*via negativa*). Eastern Christians recognize the distinction, but call the two ways more precisely and accurately cataphatic and apophatic, and prefer the latter to the former. The Western Church tends to reverse this judgement.

Via positiva proceeds by way of affirmation and describes God in terms of human attributes, raising them, of course, to an infinite power. He is love, light, life, might, majesty, mystery, and everything else that can be given a positive content. Though inexpressibly beyond all human understanding of these terms, there is still a connexion between the human significance and the divine, and the difference is quantitative rather than qualitative. Broadly, this is the biblical view, and though it lays itself open to the charge of making God in man's image, its safeguard is in the teaching that man is made in God's image, and that our virtues and graces are but the reflection of his.

Via negativa starts from the unknowability of God. Unless he should reveal himself men would know virtually nothing of him. God is 'wholly other', and qualitatively different from his creatures; they depend on him, but not he on them. Creation contributes nothing to his fulness or his happiness: he is complete in himself, and fundamentally beyond the power of any created intellect to comprehend. Any description however exalted is inevitably a human one, and because of this difference in kind can never be accurate or adequate. If we say that he is 'great' or 'most highest', or is 'a person' or is 'good', we use words which can only be properly understood in a human context, words which distinguish 'you' from 'me', and each of us from the next man. Manifestly we cannot speak of Deity like that, for the finite and temporal cannot stand over against the Infinite and Eternal. God cannot be great or high or personal or good in our sense of the words. He of whom the Positive Way would make many and glorious affirmations is so much more than these that we speak more truly when we say he is none of them, and is more worthily described negatively than positively. He cannot be understood by man's intellect. The truths of religion about him can, but not himself. When the mind faces him who is absolutely different it 'seizes up'; it becomes blank before a knowledge it can never assimilate because it can never understand the first thing about it; it enters a cloud of unknowing.

It is not very difficult to see that this way of Dionysius is negative in name only. It is because the truths about God are so overwhelmingly positive and real that we cannot describe them. But we have to try to do so, and at times the mystic will use affirmative terms, and at times negative. At no time will he say that God is unknowable, save to the power of the intellect, and then only because it is limited. God can be known by love, and by love the soul enters into union with him. The way that love is expressed and experienced is in prayer. Prayer is communion with God, leading to union.

The Mystic Way

It must not be forgotten that behind these recognizable written sources lay the vast and accumulating tradition of the Church. Part of it was written, as for example in the Scriptures, Creeds, formularies, and writings of orthodox theologians. Much of it was oral, but no less formative. The roots of Christian spirituality are deeply founded in the New Testament, even if, on occasion, they have been watered from neo-platonic wells. From the first day to this each generation has produced its outstanding saints and contemplatives, and the names of some of them have been cherished and revered. Often enough their fame has been preserved because of their writings, but this is by no means invariably the case. The memory of the Church does not depend upon literary remains, and her calendars are studded with the names of those who either did not or could not write a word.

Such catalogues, however, can do no more than represent the least part of a tithe of the untold host of Christian people of every degree of ability, culture, and temperament who have practised what Dionysius would call the threefold way of purgation, illumination, and (if so privileged) union. These devout and disciplined souls in their longing for God have always 'pressed towards the prize of his high calling in Christ Jesus', and in their urgency have contributed to the unspoken yet vital tradition of the Church. It was then as now. In this rich and growing tradition was every Christian mystic reared; from it he drew the mass of his teaching; to it in turn he applied his own distinctive insights, and added his particular emphasis. If sometimes he gave it a twist that made it look new, or if indeed he brought in something that was new, he was professedly unaware of it and would disclaim all intention of departing from the sacred deposit entrusted to the Church.

Broadly speaking, for the first thousand years Western Christendom expressed its knowledge of the spiritual life in terms of the *via positiva*. Contemplation was experienced as a revelation of light and beauty and knowledge and love and power and fulness beyond compare or description. All the characteristic features of the later mysticism (though not all its emphases) can be found in the writings of these earlier contemplatives, and there is a directness, a balance, and a wholeness about them which is not always noticeable in their medieval successors.

This positive way of describing the life of prayer was gradually altered by two major developments. One was the rise of what we know as Scholasticism, and the other was the discovery of Dionysius by the West.

The Scholastic movement, which can be said to have begun in the tenth century and to reach its full flowering with St Thomas Aquinas in the thirteenth, was a natural and, indeed, inevitable growth. It had as its aim the deeper understanding of the Christian faith by the rigorous application of certain intellectual disciplines. It defined, analysed, and coordinated the data of religion, and on the resultant system proceeded to speculate and philosophize with reverent boldness. Everything Christian came within its purview, and was integrated into one magnificent whole.

The life of prayer was subjected to such analysis and systematization. It was realized that behind the experiences which the mystics described in their halting but highly suggestive phrases lay certain common factors, and that in the early stages, at least, the majority of them walked by the same way. Not that the writing mystics themselves are systematic and analytical. There is a kind of breathlessness and untidiness about them which most effectively conveys the greatness of the experience they are struggling to express. But generally speaking – there are notable exceptions – there is no apparent system, and the ground plan has to be deduced from the finished building. Few contemplative writers, however, could remain unaffected in some way by the current theological tendency, and even a work like *The Cloud of Unknowing*, the product of a vigorous and independent mind, shows many traces of its fourteenth-century provenance, and markedly in its later chapters.

The second great influence was the discovery of Dionysius by the Western Church. Latin Christendom had, of course, known the existence of the *Mystical Theology* and his other writings; it had even paid lip service to him. But there it had stopped; his influence was negligible.

The translation of Dionysius from Greek into Latin by the Irishman Erigena in the ninth century altered the situation profoundly. Slowly but surely his teachings became known, and were accepted. His quasi-apostolic standing was unquestioned, and not until much later – in the sixteenth century, and then not universally – was he recognized as 'pseudo'. By the time *The Cloud* was written his authority on matters spiritual was paramount. The book shows his influence on every page.

Few writers on spirituality since that time have been able to resist his spell. Even in our own day when voices are at last being raised in criticism and query, Dionysius is still a very powerful force. Indeed, the indications provided by the rapidly growing interest in the ways of prayer of the Orthodox Church (Dionysian through and through) suggests that his popularity and influence will wax rather than wane.

It will not be without value to set down the broad outlines of the life of prayer as many would see it today, when the fruits of these two great movements have largely been assimilated. It will not only help us to see how *The Cloud* writings fit into the modern picture, but will also enable us to see more clearly when prayer ceases to be ordinary and becomes mystical. There are certain basic principles that we must hold on to, or it does not make sense. But grasp these, and the whole scheme becomes both profound and simple. They are these: God is essentially indescribable, being utterly beyond our power of comprehension. He is not unknowable, however, for he can be reached, known, and 'oned with' by love. This ability to love him and know him would not be possible without his prior love for us and his revelation of himself in Jesus Christ. That we are able to approach him is due to his grace or free gift.

The writers on prayer normally begin by distinguishing between *Vocal* and *Mental Prayer*; the former being prayer in which words are formed and used; the latter being prayer which takes place in the mind. It is admittedly an inadequate division, for most people most of the time think in words even if they do not use them, but it has the merit of preserving the truth that we can see facts, and see into them 'in a trembling flash' without being able or wanting to describe them. We see, we know. Mental prayer is regarded as a higher stage than vocal.

The prayers in which we use words are customarily divided into five component parts: worship, thanksgiving, confession, intercession (for other people), and petition (for oneself). Also included under the same general heading is *Ejaculatory Prayer*, short and secret words or sentences shot like an arrow up to God outside the regular times of devotion.

All forms of prayer, even mystical, could be covered by the general heading of Mental Prayer, but the word is reserved by most writers as a synonym for *Meditation*. Meditation is the deliberate, and usually systematic reflection on some truth or passage of Scripture. It has a threefold purpose: to instruct the mind, to move the will, and to warm the heart for prayer. There is a pronounced intellectual element in meditation, and it could quite easily become just an exercise of the mind ('a preaching of a sermon to oneself' as some have described it) unless there were safeguards to direct it into the channel of prayer. All systems, of course, do so direct it. There are numberless schemes for meditating which need not be gone into here. Any textbook of prayer will outline the major ones. Some of them look on paper to be very daunting indeed, but nearly all of them can be reduced quite simply to four or five basic elements, and practised by the beginner. All the mystics regard meditation as a fundamental step in the life of prayer, for it is a way of learning about God, and therefore, in the early stages, a way of hearing his voice.

Once the mind is sufficiently instructed in the things of God, and the heart turns easily towards him, meditation becomes less urgent, and indeed, unnecessary. It can even be a hindrance. For the soul who is getting to know God experimentally no longer depends upon this preliminary exercise, but can enter communion straight away. In this more intimate knowledge the freedom of the earlier stages tends to dry up, and it is sufficient to converse with God in simple phrases, sometimes often repeated. For most people it is impossible to do otherwise. A man and a woman in love with each other have a lot to say in the early stages of their courtship, but as their love deepens so the inadequacy of their thought and language about each other becomes more apparent, and they have to speak in shorter, more pregnant and meaningful phrases, but much less flowery than the earlier expressions. More would be neither sincere nor true. Something analogous characterizes the developing, simplifying prayer. The soul is now in love with God, and more tongue-tied. This stage of prayer is called *Affective*, not because the affections are aroused in an emotional way (that can happen, but it is comparatively rare) but because the expression of prayer is basically affective or loving, even when the soul feels dry and desolate.

The time may come when the soul will feel its prayer to have dried up completely, and will be bewildered that it should be so. This stage is normally regarded as the beginning of Mystical Prayer. What is happening is that the soul in its generosity is giving everything it knows to God, and seeking him and him primarily. And he is responding and has come so near that the normal apparatus of the mind cannot interpret the experience until it is adjusted to it. Its receiving set, if we can talk in pictures, is swamped by the strength of the signals it receives, and is not at once (or for a long time) able to tune in sufficiently finely to distinguish these. The result is that at this stage there is very real suffering on the part of the soul, who wants nothing but God, but can only feel desolation and dismay. This stage of wanting and not perceiving has a further significance in that it serves to strip the soul of everything that would obtrude between it and God. For though the soul might think it had given all over to God, it has still to learn that there is much yet to be surrendered. God must be loved not merely primarily but for himself alone; all between has to go. This *night of the senses*, as some call it, is due to the loving action of God, for, as we have seen, God is now more obviously taking the initiative, and assuming control. Indeed, he has been doing this all along, as the mystic always recognizes. All is 'of grace', and without God's prevenient mercy nothing in the life of prayer would be possible. But now his action is more apparent, at least to the outside observer; hitherto it has been hidden. This 'night' lasts for just so long as God wills, and, subjectively, for all the time that the soul needs such purging. It is sometimes accompanied by, and sometimes followed by a *night of the spirit* in which the soul undergoes further purification, becoming aware of its own utter worthlessness and nothingness till it is clearly resolved to serve and love God wholly and solely for himself, and not his consolations. It is not, however, all unrelieved darkness and dereliction. There are moments of light. Yet sometimes the soul loses patience, and turns back. This is the crisis hour in the life of prayer. Even when the night is at its darkest, the soul is becoming more sure of God. It does not understand, there seems nothing to live for, and yet beneath it all is this inescapable awareness of him, and the dreadful hunger for him. It is easy for the theorist to see that the soul already has him, or more accurately is his, and is being purged of all that comes between, but to the soul in this state it is nothing like so clear or certain. There is a 'groaning and a travailing in pain', but no 'earnest expectation'; only a faint hope that refuses to be quenched. It feels literally outside itself, held in a power that cannot be gainsaid; almost indeed to be the sport of this power. Nor is the soul far wrong; God is at work, and in command, and working out his, and not the soul's will.

However long delayed – and it accords seemingly with the completeness and immediacy of the soul's response, though the initiative is always God's – there is the inevitable outcome. To the dimly perceived presence of God there is an unreserved yielding and the soul begins to experience the touch of God such as it has never known before, quite indescribable, and absolutely ravishing. These 'touches of God' (it is safer to call them this rather than 'moments of vision', though any language at this time is inadequate), because they come from him, last just so long as he desires, and are experienced as and when he wills. The time and manner of their coming are quite unpredictable. All the soul can do in preparation, therefore, is to be as wholly at God's disposal as it knows how, and to rejoice that whether it has bliss or darkness, such is the will of God for it and is best.

In general it would seem that these touches of God, while they last, leave the mind and the senses comparatively free. Understandably the soul will not want to be disturbed, and body and mind will remain passive in its deep happiness. But with necessary effort the faculties can be exercised in this *Prayer of Quiet*, as some theologians call it.

It is possible for these experiences to become more intense, and frequent. *Full Union* describes the awareness of union so deep that the powers of mind are held captive by it, and enraptured. *Ecstatic Union* is deeper still, and suspends by its very intensity the bodily as well as the mental activities. The outward expressions of rapture and ecstasy tend to diminish as the soul becomes more accustomed to these visitations, and for this the mystic is profoundly grateful. For he no less than his companions is distressed at the embarrassment his trances cause, however delightful they are to him personally. Almost without exception the masters of the spiritual life warn against making ecstasy a sign of spirituality, and suggest that it should never be sought for, and discounted if it comes. Not all of the great mystics seem to have experienced these psycho-physical phenomena, and it may well be, on the human level, that the liability to such depends more on temperament and psychical make-up than on the visit of God itself. The danger of counterfeiting is too obvious to be stressed.

The *Spiritual Marriage* is the acme of mystical experience. Few reach this stage in which the soul becomes ready for the closest union of man with God possible on earth.

Human nature would not be itself if it did not try to fit these medieval works into this general pattern. Not a great deal is gained by such treatment. A fourteenth-century writer could not anticipate the systematic analyses of the sixteenth, and it is best to accept him on his own terms. His mystical experience no doubt would be basically similar, but his description of it and his thinking about it would be coloured by the psychology of his day. Herein lies his great strength, for today he is read unaffected by the technical jargon and thought forms of later years. However some persist in trying to relate the medieval to the modern, and find much to encourage them.

Thus, if they want to check the genuineness of the call to contemplation, they find it well set out in *Privy Counsel* (Chapter 11). Throughout these writings the necessary steps for spiritual development are implicit (cf. the reading, meditation, and praying of *The Cloud*, Chapter 35), and sacramental confession in particular is often referred to, getting its fullest treatment in *The Discerning of Spirits*. *Mystical Teaching* will supply the emphasis on spiritual stripping in its picture of the statue waiting to be released from its block of wood, and *Privy Counsel* will enlarge the message with its immense stress on the need for a complete forgetting, even of one's own self-awareness, before one can be vested with the grace and awareness of God's very self. It is generally held that the two Nights (of the Senses and of the Spirit) as elaborated by St John of the Cross are treated as one by the author of these works, and this view is shared by the present editor. But the bitter experiences described by St John are parallelled here by *The Cloud*'s vision of Hell, and the feeling of utter despair (Chapter 69). And the Fiend attacks the soul relentlessly (*Privy Counsel*, Chapter 5).

St John's *toda y nada* is almost the exact echo of *The Cloud*'s 'nothing which is the All' (Chapter 68). Indeed the similarity of doctrine between the two mystics, English and

Spanish, separated as they are by two centuries, and with no apparent or explicable literary connexion, is one of the minor mysteries of mysticism, and has often been commented on. Perhaps it is less mysterious than it seems, given two men of a similar cast of mind, capacity, and outlook ... and the Holy Spirit. There is no reason why he should be self-contradictory.

And though the author clearly approves of orderly spiritual development, and might even be said to endorse Richard of St Victor's classification in his version of *Benjamin Minor*, leading up as it does to ecstasy, it would not be true to say that there is undue stress on such progressive steps. It is always a 'work' (this is a key-word), but the wonderful and indescribable experience of contemplation can be had by the simplest, and that very soon. The basic requirement is acceptance of one's self, and of God as one's being. This realization involves as a logical necessity an utter determination (the 'naked intent') to reach out to the Divine Being, and to love him who is far beyond the limitations of rational thought, but who has 'first loved us'.

NOTES

Chapters and Other Matters

Two of the four works in this volume come with chapter divisions. They are *The Cloud of Unknowing* and *Mystical Teaching*. They are not part of the original text, but have been added by earlier editors. The others have no such tradition and can be sub-divided at the inclination of their readers. This subjective risk has not been taken here, though the chapters in *Privy Counsel* are based on Dom Justin McCann's suggestions, with the exception of Chapter 13 which does not seem to merit separate treatment. For *The Epistle of Prayer* the present editor has ventured to number the paragraphs, for ease of reference, and to make the pages more aesthetically acceptable.

The order in which the books are printed is a matter of personal judgement. It seems realistic to put the most important first, and to set the others according to their relative value.

Acknowledgements

Over the years a fair number of people have contributed encouragement and critical appreciation of this translation. A particular debt of gratitude is owed to Dom Augustine Morris O.S.B., until recently Abbot of Nashdom, who has always given time to make helpful suggestions and corrections. But others too have been generous in their assistance, and among them are Joyce and John Wolters, and members of the Church in Sanderstead and Newcastle, Marjorie Anderson, Bernard Hollingsworth, Peter and Marion Jackson, Kathleen Milne, Muriel Robson, and Mildred Mudie. The typing has been done by Mrs Anderson

(Sanderstead), and by Miss Robson and Mrs Mudie (New-castle), the last named making herself responsible for the cognate works. To all these, special thanks are due.

Select Bibliography

'Of making many books there is no end,' sighed the writer of Ecclesiastes (12:12). What he would have said two millennia later is anybody's guess, but his original lament could well be extended to cover the large variety of books which deal with Christian spirituality and mysticism, both medieval and modern. Most of those listed below have contributed to this present work, and gratitude therefor is hereby expressed. But the list must not be taken as exhaustive: it could have been doubled without much difficulty. Nor should the classification be regarded as definitive: the books shade into each other frequently, and many of them could appear under a different heading with equal accuracy.

THE CLOUD OF UNKNOWING, ITS COGNATES, AND ITS CONTEMPORARIES

The definitive editions of *The Cloud* and the author's other writings are the fruit of the scholarship of Dr Phyllis Hodgson. There are two volumes, each with a full and critical introduction, and excellent notes, bibliography, and vocabulary. No serious student can afford to ignore them.

Hodgson, P. *The Cloud of Unknowing*. (It includes *Privy Counsel*) E.E.T.S. and O.U.P., 1958.

Dionise Hid Divinite. (It includes *Benjamin*, the *Epistle of Prayer*, *Discretion of Stirrings*, and *Discretion of Spirits*) E.E.T.S. and O.U.P., 1958.

Other versions of *The Cloud of Unknowing*, variously

modernized and all called by its name are (in order of increasing modernization) by Evelyn Underhill (London, 1912), Justin McCann (London, 1924), and a 'member of the Pendle Hill Community' (New York, 1948). The publication of the Penguin edition stimulated fresh interest in *The Cloud*, and there is a vigorous, free translation both of *The Cloud* and *Privy Counsel* by W. Johnston (New York, 1971). An excellent French translation, *Le Nuage de l'Inconnaissance*, was made by M. Noetinger (Tours, 1925).

Modernized versions of some of the cognate works are:

Gardner, J. E. G. *The Cell of Self-Knowledge*. London, 1910.

Walsh, J. *A Letter of Private Direction*. London, 1963.

Two important commentaries of *The Cloud* writings have appeared since 1961:

Johnston, W. *The Mysticism of the Cloud of Unknowing*. New York, 1967.

Nieva, C. S. *This Transcending God*. London, 1971 (a doctoral thesis, slightly fussy and ill-arranged, but thorough-going).

Penguin Books have published in current English some of the medieval contemporaries of *The Cloud*:

Richard Rolle *The Fire of Love*, 1971.

Julian of Norwich *Revelations of Divine Love*, 1966.

Walter Hilton *The Ladder of Perfection*, 1957.

The great book on Rolle is *Writings ascribed to Richard Rolle* by H. E. Allen (New York, 1966), and on Julian it is probably that by Paul Molinari, *Julian of Norwich* (London, 1958).

Descriptive accounts of all these books will be found in many modern writings. Among the most accessible are:

Colledge, E. *The Mediaeval Mystics of England*. London, 1962.

Inge, W. R. *Studies of English Mystics*. London, 1906.

Knowles, D. *The English Mystical Tradition*. London, 1964.

Pepler, C. *The English Religious Heritage*. London, 1958.

Renaudin, P. *Quatre Mystiques Anglais*. Paris, 1945.

Sitwell, G. *Medieval Spiritual Writers*. London, 1961.

Thornton, M. *English Spirituality*. London, 1963.

Underhill, E. *The Mystics of the Church*. London, 1933.
                    Mixed Pastures. London, 1933.

Walsh, J. *Pre-Reformation English Spirituality*. London, 1965.

CHRISTIAN MYSTICISM

There is still nothing quite as good as Evelyn Underhill's *Mysticism*, published in 1911, but the books below are all important:

Butler, C. *Western Mysticism*. London, 1958.

Happold, F. C. *Mysticism*. Harmondsworth, 1963.

Inge, W. R. *Christian Mysticism*. London, 1899.

Kirchberger, C. *Richard of St Victor: Selected Writings on Contemplation*. London, 1957.

Kirk, K. E. *The Vision of God*. London, 1931.

Lossky, V. *The Mystical Theology of the Eastern Church*. London, 1957.

Peers, A. *The Complete Works of St John of the Cross*. London, 1935.

Rolt, C. E. *Dionysius the Areopagite*. London, 1920.

Spencer, S. *Mysticism in World Religion*. Harmondsworth, 1963.

Trethowan, I. *Mysticism and Theology*. London, 1975.

PRAYER AND THE SPIRITUAL LIFE

On this subject a vast literature accumulates, with books

to support and guide at every stage of development or need. None of these listed here is unimportant, and most of them provide a balanced and comprehensive account of its growth and depth.

von Balthasar, H. U. *Prayer.* London, 1973.

Garrigou-Lagrange, R. M. *Christian Perfection and Contemplation.* London, 1949.

Graham, A. *Contemplative Christianity.* London, 1975.

de Guibert, J. *The Theology of the Spiritual Life.* London, 1954.

Harton, F. P. *The Elements of the Spiritual Life.* London, 1932.

Johnston, W. *Silent Music.* London, 1974.

Leclercq, J. *et al. La Spiritualité du Moyen Age.* Paris, 1960.

English translation, *Spirituality of the Middle Ages.* London, 1968.

Merton, T. *Contemplation in a World of Action.* London, 1971.

Northcott, H. *The Venture of Prayer.* London, 1950.

Poulain, A. *The Graces of Interior Prayer.* London, 1912.

Tanquerey, A. *The Spiritual Life.* Tournai, 1948.

Thornton, M. *Prayer: A New Encounter.* London, 1972.

Ward, J. N. *The Use of Praying.* London, 1967.

BACKGROUND BOOKS

It seems that great writing can persist only if it is true to deep human experience. *The Cloud* and its cognates pass such a test. Their greatness stands out even more starkly when they are seen in their historical, social, and religious context. The following books give fascinating and readable background information about the Middle Ages.

Bishop, M. *The Penguin Book of the Middle Ages.* Harmondsworth, 1968.

Clay, R. M. *The Hermits and Anchorites of England*. London, 1914.

Darwin, F. D. S. *The English Medieval Recluse*. London, 1944.

Deanesly, M. *A History of the Medieval Church*. London, 1925.

Knowles, D. *Evolution of Medieval Thought*. London, 1962.

Pantin, W. A. *The English Church in the Fourteenth Century*. Cambridge, 1955.

Sumption, J. *Pilgrimage*. London, 1975.

Southern, R. W. *The Making of the Middle Ages*. London, 1953.

INTRODUCTION TO THE CLOUD OF UNKNOWING

Leading Ideas

OUTLINE

For all its ease of style *The Cloud of Unknowing* is a difficult book to analyse. Its author had a clear idea of what he wanted to say, but no formulated plan for putting it over. He writes easily and fluently and at times with quiet beauty, but one is left with the impression that he unfolds his theme as it comes to his mind, rather than follows a pre-arranged scheme. This is not to say there is no sense of development in the book, or no underlying unity that holds it together, but it is a warning to the reader to be prepared for deviations from the straight ascent of the Holy Mount, as the author invites him to turn aside to inspect particular objects on the way.

The key to the understanding of the book is to be found in the first three chapters, and all the rest is in the nature of comment and expansion. In these opening pages we are reminded that God in his love is calling his young disciple to a higher stage in the spiritual life. And though he does not deserve so great a privilege he must respond to it with the utmost diligence and humility. Basically his attitude must be one of longing desire and love for God. It will involve spiritual watchfulness, a forgetting of the past, a dedicated will, and a determination to reach out to God in the intellectual darkness of the *cloud of unknowing*. Chapter 4 stresses the fact that the work of contemplation is initially God's, and that ours is that of a responsive will, and that this work of grace can be effected in a very brief time. Chapters 5–12 deal with the inability of the intellect to reach God, and the various problems which arise as thought and memory have to be put away under the 'Cloud of Forgetting'. Love is the way of union with God, and the next thirteen chapters mention the fruits of such love, particularly the virtues of humility and charity, exemplified in the story of Martha and Mary; a popular theme with mystical writers, and handled here with much skill and delicate insight. But contemplation can be very hard work, and how hard is shown in Chapters 26–33, where the author writes usefully and originally on sin, and ways to overcome its assaults. From Chapter 34 onwards some of the characteristics of the contemplative life are set down: its prior disciplines, the instantaneous and embracing nature of its prayer and meditation, its need for complete generosity of response and holy indifference to rules and regulations, its call for complete self-forgetting, even to the extent of awareness of oneself. The eagerness of spirit which is the basis of contemplation must be a general eagerness with its desire unformulated in precise and particular terms. Though spiritual consolations are possible they must not be sought, but treated rather with indifference and even with suspicion. Throughout his book the writer has been concerned with the possible misinterpretations of his words, and Chapters 51–61 are primarily concerned with this danger. His sense of humour observable throughout the book here comes out into the open with some devastating pictures of the pseudo-contemplative. An excursion into medieval psychology, more useful, perhaps, for the young disciple then than for us now, and of relatively little interest, follows from Chapters 62–5, and they still echo the author's fear of misunderstanding. With the spiritual nature of contemplation now safeguarded, we are plunged into the All and the Unknowing from Chapters 67–70 in as fine a passage of mystical writing as one could wish to read. Old Testament types of contemplative experience, and a surprisingly modern display of understanding tolerance are the basis of Chapters 71-4, and the last chapter of all fulfils the promise of the Introduction to give signs whereby it can be known whether the call to this work is coming from God or not.

GRACE

Though the Christian Church is not committed to the full-blooded acceptance of the Dionysian incomprehensibility of God, she unhesitatingly declares that unless God should reveal himself we should know very little about him, and certainly be unable to contemplate him. But she also confidently affirms that God has revealed himself, primarily through the Hebrews, and supremely through Jesus Christ. And because of this gracious act, man may come to trust and know and love, and ultimately to see and unite with him. The Church exists, she believes, for this very purpose, that in her and through her the freely given help of God (in other words, his grace) may enable man to achieve his true end, God himself.

The Cloud of Unknowing, this 'book of contemplation' springing from the Christian faith, is at pains to emphasize that the initiative is always with God, and that only by his grace may the soul contemplate him. The very 'work' that the response to God's call involves is only possible through his sustaining power. He 'made thee and wrought thee ... and bought thee ... and kindled thy desire ... and led thee' (Chapter 1) and he continues his work until that day when 'thou attainest to come thither by grace whither thou mayest not come by nature, that is to say, to be oned to God in spirit and in love and in accordance of will' (Chapter 67). From beginning to end it is all 'of grace'. It would be tedious and unnecessary to labour this point, for the reader can easily discover it for himself. It is sufficient to say that in the text of seventy-five short chapters, the word 'grace' and its cognates are found over ninety times, and that this number is in addition to the many other references to the providential and prevenient work of God. It is summed up neatly in Chapter 34: 'For why, that is the work of only God, specially wrought in what soul that him liketh without any desert of the same soul ... Let that thing do with thee and lead thee whereso it list. Let it be the worker, and thou but the sufferer ... be thou but the tree, and let it be the wright: be thou but the house, and let it be the husbandman dwelling therein. Be blind in this time, and shear away covetise of knowing, for it will more let thee than help thee. It sufficeth enough unto thee, that thou feelest thee stirred likingly, with a thing thou wottest never what, else that in this stirring thou hast no special thought of anything under God; and that thine intent be nakedly directed unto God.'

THE NAKED INTENT WHICH IS LONGING LOVE

But though this grace of God is, in theological terms, prevenient, habitual, and sufficient, it is not irresistible. There has to be the cooperation of the soul, and without it God is powerless to raise it to contemplation. Normally the soul is prepared for this privilege by its prior reading, meditations, and prayers – all assumed in *The Cloud* (Chapter 35) – and by the time the call comes the spade work has been done.

The response that is needed is, as the quotation above reminded us, 'that thine intent be nakedly directed unto God'. This 'naked intent' which is often spoken of in the book is an untranslatable term, and has different nuances in different contexts. Basically it is the deliberate purpose of the heart to love God, a purpose which nothing is allowed to deflect, and which, even when stripped of its attendant memories and pleasures, remains unalterably turned towards him. 'Look that nothing live in thy working mind but a naked intent stretching into God' (Ep. Privy Counsel, Chapter 1).

In several places this 'intent' is very closely associated with 'longing' and 'love', and at times seems to pass over into them. 'Cease never in thine intent; but beat ever more on this cloud of unknowing that is betwixt thee and thy God with a sharp dart of longing love, and loathe for to think on aught under God, and go not thence for anything that befalleth' (Chapter 12). This longing love is of vital importance, and must be acquired before the work can begin, and progress be made (Chapter 3). Once love has sprung, the soul can 'press' lovingly upon God. Love holds the key to contemplation. Through love God is known, not through the intellect: 'He may well be loved, but not thought. By love may he be gotten and holden; but by thought never' (Chapter 6). Intellectually the soul is blank in contemplation, and it is in this blankness of ignorance, or *cloud of unknowing*, that God is 'known' by outreaching love (Chapter 3 and *passim*). The soul must concentrate on God as he is in himself, wholly and solely; not on his goods or his attributes, the consideration of which would detract from the purity of contemplation.

Not surprisingly this loving attention to God has most useful by-products. It is, for example, the way, and the only way, by which sin can be totally destroyed. Sin cannot live in the presence of God any more than night in the presence of day. This is by itself 'the only work that destroyeth the root and ground of sin' (Chapter 12).

And it is the source of goodness, and produces the twin foundation virtues of humility and charity. In a section of singular perception and charm, the author expounds the story of Martha and Mary (Chapters 16-23). He draws a great deal more out of it than would be permitted today; but two of his points are surely sound when he says that love procured Mary's (i.e. the contemplative's) forgiveness, and that it heightened her humble penitence: 'She had a more hearty sorrow, a more doleful desire, and a more deep sighing, and more she languished, yea almost to the death, for lacking of love, although she had full much love ... than she had for any remembrance of her sins' (Chapter 16).

This love for God, so urgent and so necessary, spreads over to all his creatures, and all are loved for his sake. It matters not whether they are friend or foe: 'All shall be loved plainly and nakedly for God' (Chapter 25). The burden of the whole book is that we 'press' upon him with 'longing love', and this 'meek stirring of love in thine heart' is 'nought else but a good and according will unto God, and a manner of well-pleasedness and gladness that thou feelest in thy will of all that he doth. Such a good will is the substance of all perfection.' Everything 'hangs on this good will' (Chapter 49). *The Cloud* is as clear as the most up-to-date writer on spirituality that the concurrence of the will is essential.

On almost every page the book is concerned with the soul's love for God, and it characteristically sums it up in a memorable passage: 'If thee list have this intent lapped and folden in one word ... take thee but a little word of one syllable ... Such a word is this word LOVE. Fasten this word to thine heart ... With this word thou shalt beat on this cloud and this darkness above thee. With this word thou shalt sink down all manner of thought under the cloud of forgetting' (Chapter 7).

THE HARDNESS OF THE WAY

The author almost invariably describes contemplation as

'work', as reference to the original text will show. This emphasis has led some to suppose that the kind of contemplation taught here is what theologians today would call 'acquired', that is, a state of prayer which is induced by the efforts of the soul, and not 'infused' (or given) by God who himself takes hold of the soul and shows it something of his glory. But there can be little doubt that the author, unaware of these later distinctions and refinements, is in fact teaching infused contemplation, as closer attention to the text will reveal.

But it is in this accent on work that *The Cloud* stresses the fact that contemplation makes demands, and involves discipline and hardship. The author is no Quietist who sits down and expects God to do it all; he knows the neophyte has got to work, and keep on working. And God will work with him.

We have seen that he takes for granted the foundation work of the prayer life, and therefore begins by reminding the young man that contemplation can only be in the *cloud of unknowing*, that darkness of intellectual ignorance which shrouds God, and which is impenetrable save to the constant pressure of love. The rethinking that the acceptance of this blind loving involves is not easy, but it is simplicity itself compared with the accompanying insistence that all thinking and memory have to be 'put down' under a *cloud of forgetting*. 'A full great travail' he rightly calls it, and 'this travail is all in treading down the remembrance of all the creatures that ever God made, and in holding them under the *cloud of forgetting*' (Chapter 26). Here again there has to be considerable adjustment of thought, for 'all the creatures that ever he made' include the holiest and most helpful meditations upon God that can possibly be conceived (Chapter 5). Even the awareness of oneself has to go, which difficult feat is achieved by the quiet, deep sorrow that is caused by the consideration that one exists over against God (Chapter 44). And for one whose religion has hitherto been largely a matter of rule, the unexpectedness and freedom of the contemplative life (Chapter 42) take no little time for assimilation.

But in addition to the mental readjustment there are the constant attacks of the world, the flesh, and the devil to cope with, any one of which may capsize the over-eager or impatient disciple. 'The world' scorns, criticizes, and sometimes actively opposes. But since it does not understand the first thing about this sort of life, it may be excused. 'The flesh' rears its ugly head in pride at the call received or at the progress made, and hangs it in despair at the magnitude of the difficulties encountered. Sometimes it misunderstands the whole business, and, aided and abetted by the Fiend, counterfeits and perverts it. There are some extremely penetrating caricatures of pseudo-contemplatives, drawn not without a touch of malice, which enliven the second half of the book, and condition us for the more solid theological teaching that follows. The assurance is given that though 'the devil' seeks to thwart the neophyte at every turn, his power progressively declines as awareness of God deepens. From the first the would-be contemplative has got to be on guard (Chapter 2).

The road winds uphill all the way, even to the very end. Some, far advanced in the arts of contemplation, withdraw because of 'the greatness of the pain they feel, and for lacking of comfort' (Chapter 69). A little more perseverance would have saved them. The story of Moses is held up as the example of the difficulties that must be endured, and for the encouragement of those who, with similar 'great long travail', climb up 'to the top of the mountain and dwell there and work in a cloud abiding unto the day that our Lord might vouchsafe to show' himself (Chapter 71).

There is unfailing need for resolution and hard work.

But it is not all hard slogging. For most people the difficulties lighten appreciably as they persevere (Chapter 26), and unsought, but not unwanted, consolations ravish and refresh the soul, who must, however, be on constant guard against them, as in too large doses they are enervating (Chapter 48). It would be completely false if we were left with the idea that it was all hard grind always. In one sense it is, but for a great many the example of the contemplative is not that of Moses but of Aaron, who 'had it in his power ... for to see It[1] in the Temple within the veil as often as he liked to enter'. And even poor Moses who was able to contemplate 'first but seldom, and not without great travail' came later to have the Vision as often as he wanted (Chapter 71). The whole message of *The Cloud* is one of great hope.

As a pendant it might be mentioned that in two places (Chapters 54, 61) it is pointed out that a man becomes much more worth knowing when he is a contemplative! However rugged of feature, people are 'suddenly and graciously changed' so that men are glad to have their company, and are 'holpen by grace unto God in their presence'. They become poised and cheerful, and able to mix with 'accustomed sinners' without being contaminated, and, indeed, attracting such to a godly life. They are unaffected, natural, wise, and serious, and their very bodies tend to take on a new carriage, manly and upright. 'Thus it is most seemly to be.'

SIN

As a general rule the habitual sinner finds the contemplative life much more difficult than do others. This, for most of us, would seem too obvious to be worth mentioning,

1. i.e. the Ark, symbol of the Presence of God.

but then we would not be sharing the viewpoint of the author, who, like the director of souls he is, immediately goes on to say that often in his experience those 'that have been horrible and accustomed sinners come sooner to the perfection of this work than those that have been none' (Chapter 29).

His treatment of sin is orthodox and unexceptionable, but in some respects it may seem fresh and unusual to modern readers.

Those of us who are ready to accept with him the Church's way of confession have a tendency to think that if our mortification and penitence were of a sufficiently high order our sinful desires would be conquered, one day if not sooner. *The Cloud* brushes all this brusquely aside: 'Fast thou never so much, wake thou never so long, rise thou never so early, lie thou never so hard, wear thou never so sharp; yea, and if it were lawful to do – as it is not – put thou out thine eyes, cut thou out thy tongue of thy mouth, stop thou thine ears and thy nose never so fast, though thou shear away thy members, and do all the pain to thy body that thou mayest or canst think: all this would help thee right nought. Yet will the stirring and rising of sin be in thee' (Chapter 12). It is the same with penitence: there is little it may do without the positive 'blind stirring of love'. The only infallible way of dealing with sin to ensure its destruction root and crop is to contemplate God. In his presence it shrivels and dies: 'For in this work a soul drieth up in it all the root and the ground of sin that will always live in it after confession' (Chapter 28).

This is the same teaching that we find in all the great writing mystics, and indeed in the New Testament, which, while it recognizes that Christians can sin, and therefore need forgiveness, also holds that 'whosoever abideth in him (i.e. Christ) sinneth not' (I John. 3:6, 9; 5:18). It is a truth not often proclaimed today.

The Cloud's handling of temptation, and the Christian's resistance to it, is striking. After saying, most sensibly, that all memories of past sins are to be firmly suppressed, it goes on to suggest 'two ghostly devices that be helpful' in dealing with temptation. The first is 'to try to look as it were over their shoulders, seeking another thing: the which thing is God'. In other words, we should studiously ignore the temptation, and concentrate on God. This is recognized to be not always possible, and a second 'device' is put forward, which, on the surface, appears to be extremely risky: 'When thou feelest that thou mayest in no wise put them down, cower thou down under them as a caitiff and a coward overcome in battle, and think that it is but a folly to strive any longer with them, and therefore thou yieldest thee to God in the hands of thine enemies' (Chapter 32). The subsequent stress that 'good heed' be paid to this device that it be 'truly conceived' hints at an uneasy fear of possible misapprehension. The underlying idea seems to be that when temptation is unavoidable and overwhelming the contemplative should completely relax in the midst of it all, and yield himself unreservedly to God, who will then 'mightily descend to venge thee of thine enemies, for to take thee up, and cherishingly dry thy ghostly eyes' (Chapter 32).

This book abounds in terse and memorable sayings, and each regular reader will have his own collection of them. Probably in every such list the phrase 'Mean by sin, a lump' (Chapter 36) will feature, for it is a characteristic thought of the book. The author, unlike some later theologians, does not deal with sins one by one, for the individual consideration of each would not only interfere with the soul's 'naked intent unto God' but might well lead to further sin. All must go into the *cloud of forgetting*. That does not imply that sin can be dismissed as of no account. On the contrary, the awareness of sin in the contemplative must be, and will be, continual until those times of vision when only God is seen. But such sin is not to be analysed or particularized, but regarded as a whole, 'the which lump is none other thing than thyself' (Chapter 43). This identification in general terms of the soul with sin will produce certain results: it will bring a fresh sense of the goodness and mercy of God; it will help to keep the soul humble; and it will cause such searching and silent sorrow that the consciousness of separate existence over against God will ultimately be washed away (Chapter 44).

CONTEMPLATION

The title of the book tells us a great deal about its theme and purpose: 'a book of contemplation, the which is called *The Cloud of Unknowing*, in the which a soul is oned with God'. Even in these days of widespread interest in Christian mysticism there is still much haziness about contemplation itself, and a word of explanation may be of use at the outset.

Contemplation is not the pleasant reaction to a celestial sunset, nor is it the perpetual twitter of heavenly birdsong. It is not even an emotion. It is the awareness of God, known and loved at the core of one's being.

In this awareness there may be no overtone of beauty, nor indeed any sort of pleasurable response at all – at least in some of the stages of the spiritual life. For though it can become so vivid as to transport and to transfix, it can for long periods be faint almost to the point of imperceptibility. And when it does communicate itself through our emotions it is as likely to awe and humble as to entrance and exalt, to daunt and bemuse as to allure and enlighten. If at times it seems to go softly, it is, in fact, never static, but living and growing; and it has a way of taking such hold of the willing soul that all life is pervaded with its indefinable, inescapable quality, and orientated, the soul feels, to its true end.

But always it is this basic sense of 'otherness' to which the soul turns as to its home, and without which it finds life insupportable.

No description of the bliss of contemplation is possible: its nature is such that it is unspeakable. Even if it were permissible to speak of it, no words could be found. So mystical writers in general do no more than hint at this glory; they are content to describe the path to the Heavenly City, the pitfalls to avoid, the obstacles to surmount, the training to undergo, the mists to grope through. The author of *The Cloud* does the same. He gives a map of the way, his way, with great and attractive simplicity; the snags and the needs are indicated, and the methods to avoid the one and implement the other are set out. On occasion, however, he gives some suggestion of the splendour that is there waiting to be revealed. Thus: 'Then will he sometimes peradventure send out a beam of ghostly light, piercing this cloud of unknowing that is betwixt thee and him: and shew thee some of his privity, the which man may not, nor cannot speak. Then shalt thou feel thine affection inflamed with the fire of his love, far more than I can tell thee, or may or will at this time. For of that work that falleth to only God, dare I not take upon me to speak with my blabbering fleshly tongue' (Chapter 26). And though as a general rule consolations are to be distrusted, when he chooses God gives 'full wonderful sweetness and comforts' (Chapter 48). Ecstasy is not unknown (Chapter 71) though it is not described. But by and large 'the over-abundant love and the worthiness of God in himself, in beholding of the which all nature quaketh, all clerks be fools, and all saints and angels be blind' (Chapter 13) can only be known in the *cloud of unknowing*.

But if the glory of contemplation is properly beyond the power of the human pen, the life of contemplation is not, and in three chapters, 68–70, there is set out with such lucidity as may be the 'Nought' which is the 'All'.

God is 'an unmade, ghostly thing'. We, on the other hand, are created, and not wholly spiritual. By our very nature we have to think in human, created terms. It is impossible to do otherwise, yet it is not until we have put them all aside, and have been prepared and purified by grace, that we can see that the Nought and the Nowhere to which our journey has brought us is the presence of God himself. For he is No-thing, and No-where. The very 'unknowing', 'full blind and full dark', is the knowing of him in this life, and is caused by 'abundance of ghostly light'. And the life of contemplation is just this unknowing knowing, this blind seeing, this presence which is unfelt . . . the earnest of the unmentionable, ineffable glory which is to come.

'Therefore get this gift whoso by grace get may!'

A BOOK ON CONTEMPLATION

CALLED

THE CLOUD OF UNKNOWING

IN WHICH CLOUD A SOUL IS UNITED WITH

GOD

GOD

unto whom all hearts are open,
unto whom all wills do speak,
from whom no secret thing is hidden,
I beseech thee
so to cleanse the purpose of my heart
with the unutterable gift of thy grace
that I may perfectly love thee,
and worthily praise thee.

AMEN

PROLOGUE

In the Name of the Father
and of the Son
and of the Holy Ghost

I CHARGE and beg you, with all the strength and power that love can bring to bear, that whoever you may be who possess this book (perhaps you own it, or are keeping it, carrying it, or borrowing it) you should, quite freely and of set purpose, neither read, write, or mention it to anyone, nor allow it to be read, written, or mentioned by anyone unless that person is in your judgement really and wholly determined to follow Christ perfectly. And to follow him not only in the active life, but to the utmost height of the contemplative life that is possible for a perfect soul in a mortal body to attain by the grace of God. And he should be, in your estimation, one who has for a long time been doing all that he can to come to the contemplative life by virtue of his active life. Otherwise the book will mean nothing to him.

Moreover I charge you and beg you, by the authority that love gives, that if any shall read, write, or mention this book, or hear it read or mentioned, you should charge them (as I do you) to take time over their reading, speaking, writing, or hearing. For there may be some matter at, say, the beginning or in the middle which is left in the air, or not fully explained in that particular context. If it is not dealt with there, perhaps it is soon after, or by the end of the book. If a man saw the matter only partially, he might easily go wrong. Therefore, to avoid this error, for yourself as well as for them, I pray you for love's sake to do what I tell you.

I do not mind at all if the loud-mouthed, or flatterers, or the mock-modest, or fault-finders, gossips, tittle-tattlers, talebearers, or any sort of grumbler, never see this book. I have never meant to write for them. So they can keep out of it. And so can all those learned men (and unlearned too) who are merely curious. Even if they are good men judged from the 'active' standpoint, all this will mean nothing to them. But it will mean something to those who, though 'active' according to their outward mode of life, are, by the inner working of the Spirit of God – his judgements are unsearchable – disposed towards contemplation. Not continually, maybe, as in the case of true contemplatives, but now and then willing to share in the deep things of contemplation. If such people see this book, by the grace of God they should be much inspired by it.

There are seventy-five chapters in this book. The last chapter of all gives definite tokens by which the soul may surely know whether God is calling him to this work or not.

LIST OF CHAPTERS

17. *The true contemplative does not concern himself with the active life, nor with what is said or done to him, nor does he refute his detractors.*

18. *To this day actives complain of contemplatives, as Martha did of Mary. Ignorance is the cause.*

19. *The author's excuse for teaching that all contemplatives should fully exonerate actives who speak or work against them.*

20. *The goodness of God Almighty who answers on behalf of those who will not leave loving him.*

21. *The true exposition of this Gospel sentence 'Mary hath chosen the best part'.*

22. *Christ's wonderful love for Mary, type of the converted sinner called to contemplation.*

23. *God answers and provides for those who for love of him will not provide for themselves.*

24. *What love is, and how it is truly and perfectly summed up in contemplation.* How contemplative people should live.

25. *At this time a perfect soul is not concerned with any one in particular.*

26. *Contemplation is very hard work apart from God's special grace, or ordinary grace and long practice. What is the soul's part, and what God's, in contemplation.*

27. *Who should engage in this work of grace.*

28. *No one should presume to become a contemplative until his conscience has been duly cleansed from his sinful deeds.*

29. *A man must continually exercise himself in this work, enduring its suffering and judging no one.*

30. *Who can blame or judge the faults of others.*

31. *How the beginner should deal with his thoughts and sinful impulses.*

32. *Two spiritual stratagems which may help the beginner.*

52. *How presumptuous young disciples understand* IN; *the resultant errors.*

53. *Various unfortunate consequences follow those who are false contemplatives.*

54. *Contemplation makes a man wise and attractive, both in body and soul.*

55. *The error of those who fervently and without due discretion reprove sin.*

56. *Those who rely on their own intellectual resources, and on human knowledge rather than on the teaching of Holy Church, are deceived.*

57. *How presumptuous young disciples misunderstand* UP; *the resultant errors.*

58. *St Martin and St Stephen are not to be taken as examples of literal looking upwards in prayer.*

59. *Nor is the Ascension of Christ such an example. Time, place, and body must be forgotten in contemplation.*

60. *The high way, and the quickest, to heaven is run by desire and not feet.*

61. *All material things are subject to spiritual, and according to natural order are determined by them and not conversely.*

62. *How to know when spiritual working is beneath, or outside, or level with, or within oneself, and when it is above one and under God.*

63. *The faculties of the soul. Mind is the principal power, and embraces all the others.*

64. *The two other principal faculties are reason and will; how sin has affected their working.*

65. *Imagination is the first secondary faculty; how its working and obedience to reason has been affected by sin.*

66. *Sensuality is the other secondary faculty; how its working and obedience to will has been affected by sin.*

My friend in God,
I earnestly beg you to look most attentively to the way and
the method of your vocation. And give God heartfelt
thanks, so that you, by the help of his grace, may stand
without flinching in the state, and stage, and manner of life
that you have wholeheartedly entered upon, against all the
wiles and assaults of your physical and spiritual foes, and
may win through to the crown of everlasting life.

AMEN

MY FRIEND IN GOD

I IT seems to me, in my rough and ready way, that there are four states or kinds of Christian life, and they are these: Common, Special, Solitary, and Perfect. Three of them may be begun and ended in this life; the fourth, by the grace of God, may be begun here, but it goes on for ever in the bliss of Heaven! And just as you will notice that I have set these four in a certain sequence (Common, Special, Solitary, Perfect) so I think that our Lord in his great mercy has called you in the same order and in the same way, leading you on to himself by your heart-felt desire.

For you are well aware that, when you were in the Common state of the Christian life, living with your friends in the world, God, through his everlasting love (which made and fashioned you when you were nothing, and then, when you were lost with Adam, bought you with the price of his precious blood) would not allow you to live the kind of life that was so far away from him. In that most gracious way of his, he kindled your desire for himself, and bound you to him by the chain of such longing, and thus led you to that more Special life, a servant among his own special servants. He did this that you might learn to be more especially his and to live more spiritually than ever you could have done in the common state of life.

And there is more: it appears that he is not content to leave you just there – such is the love of his heart which he has always had for you – but in his own delightful and gracious way he has drawn you to this third stage, the Solitary. It is in this state that you will learn to take your first loving steps to the life of Perfection, the last stage of all.

2 PAUSE for a moment, you wretched weakling, and take stock of yourself. Who are you, and what have you deserved, to be called like this by our Lord? How sluggish and slothful the soul that does not respond to Love's attraction and invitation!

At this stage, wretched man, you must keep an eye on your enemy. You must not think yourself any holier or better because of the worthiness of your calling, and because you live the solitary life. Rather the opposite: you are even more wretched and cursed unless you are doing your very best to live answerably to your calling, helped as you are by grace and direction. You ought to be all the more humble and loving to your spiritual husband who is Almighty God, King of Kings and Lord of Lords and yet has so humbly come down to your level, and so graciously chosen you out of his flock to be one of his 'specials', and has set you in rich pasture to be fed with the sweet food of his love, a foretaste of your inheritance in the Kingdom of Heaven.

So go on, I beg you, with all speed. Look forward, not backward. See what you still lack, not what you have already; for that is the quickest way of getting and keeping humility. Your whole life now must be one of longing, if you are to achieve perfection. And this longing must be in the depths of your will, put there by God, with your consent. But a word of warning: he is a jealous lover, and will brook no rival; he will not work in your will if he has not sole charge; he does not ask for help, he asks for you. His will is that you should look at him, and let him have his way. You must, however, guard your spiritual windows and doorways against enemy attacks. If you are willing to do this, you need only to lay hold upon God humbly in prayer, and he will soon help you. Lay hold of him then,

Very majestic view of God.

and see how you fare. God is ready when you are, and is *
waiting for you.

* But what am I to do, you say, and how am I to 'lay
hold'?

3 LIFT up your heart to God with humble love: and *prayer*
mean God himself, and not what you get out of him.
Indeed, hate to think of anything but God himself, so that
nothing occupies your mind or will but only God. Try to *good to do*
forget all created things that he ever made, and the purpose *in meditation*
behind them, so that your thought and longing do not turn
or reach out to them either in general or in particular. Let
them go, and pay no attention to them. It is the work of
the soul that pleases God most. All saints and angels rejoice
over it, and hasten to help it on with all their might. All
the fiends, however, are furious at what you are doing, and
try to defeat it in every conceivable way. Moreover, the
whole of mankind is wonderfully helped by what you are
doing, in ways you do not understand. Yes, the very souls
in purgatory find their pain eased by virtue of your work.
And in no better way can you yourself be made clean or
virtuous than by attending to this. Yet it is the easiest work
of all when the soul is helped by grace and has a conscious
longing. And it can be achieved very quickly. Otherwise
it is hard and beyond your powers.

Do not give up then, but work away at it till you have
this longing. When you first begin, you find only darkness,
and as it were a cloud of unknowing. You don't know what
this means except that in your will you feel a simple steadfast intention reaching out towards God. Do what you will,
this darkness and this cloud remain between you and God,
and stop you both from seeing him in the clear light of

rational understanding, and from experiencing his loving sweetness in your affection. Reconcile yourself to wait in this darkness as long as is necessary, but still go on longing after him whom you love. For if you are to feel him or to see him in this life, it must always be in this cloud, in this darkness. And if you will work hard at what I tell you, I believe that through God's mercy you will achieve this very thing.

patience in prayer

4 So that you may make no mistake, or go wrong in this matter, let me tell you a little more about it as I see it.

This work does not need a long time for its completion. Indeed, it is the shortest work that can be imagined! It is no longer, no shorter, than one atom, which as a philosopher of astronomy will tell you is the smallest division of time. It is so small that it cannot be analysed: it is almost beyond our grasp. Yet it is as long as the time of which it has been written, 'All the time that is given to thee, it shall be asked of thee how thou hast spent it.' And it is quite right that you should have to give account of it. It is neither shorter nor longer than a single impulse of your will, the chief part of your soul.

give a little time back to God thru contemplation

For there can be as many movements or desires of your will within the hour as there are atoms of time. If grace had restored your soul to the state of Adam's soul before the Fall, you would be in control of your every impulse. None would go astray, but all would reach out to the sovereign of all desires, the peak of all that can be willed, God himself.

For he comes down to our level, adapting his Godhead to our power to comprehend. Our soul has some affinity with him, of course, because we have been created in his image and likeness. Only he himself is completely and

KNOWING BY LOVING

utterly sufficient to fulfil the will and longing of our souls.
Nothing else can. The soul, when it is restored by grace, is
made wholly sufficient to comprehend him fully by love.
He cannot be comprehended by our intellect or any man's –
or any angel's for that matter. For both we and they are
created beings. But only to our intellect is he incompre-
hensible: not to our love.

All rational beings, angels and men, possess two faculties,
the power of knowing and the power of loving. To the
first, to the intellect, God who made them is forever unknowable, but to the second, to love, he is completely
knowable, and that by every separate individual. So much
so that one loving soul by itself, through its love, may
know for itself him who is incomparably more than sufficient to fill all souls that exist. This is the everlasting miracle
of love, for God always works in this fashion, and always
will. Consider this, if by God's grace you are able to. To
know it for oneself is endless bliss; its contrary is endless
pain.

If any man were so refashioned by the grace of God that
he heeded every impulse of his will, he would never be
without some sense of the eternal sweetness, even in this
life, nor without its full realization in the bliss of heaven.
So do not be surprised if I urge you on. It is this very thing
that man would be doing today if he had not sinned – as
you will be hearing later. For this was man made, and all
else was made to help him achieve this end. It is by this that
man shall be restored. And it is because he does not heed
that a man falls ever more deeply into sin, becoming ever
more estranged from God. Yet on the other hand, it is by
constantly heeding and attending to this very thing and
nothing else that a man gets more free from sin, and nearer
to God.

So be very careful how you spend time. There is nothing

63

more precious. In the twinkling of an eye heaven may be won or lost. God shows that time is precious, for he never gives two moments of time side by side, but always in succession. To do otherwise he would have to alter the whole course of creation. Time is made for man, not man for time. And God, who orders nature, fitted time in with the nature of man – and man's natural impulses occur one at a time. Man will have no excuse before God at the Day of Judgement when he gives account of how he spent his time. He cannot say: 'Thou dost give two times at once, when I have but one impulse at the same moment.'

But now you are anxious, and say, 'What am I to do? If what you are saying is true, how am I to give account of each moment of time? Here am I, twenty-four years old, altogether heedless of time! Were I to amend straight away, you know perfectly well from what you have already written that neither in nature nor in grace are there any moments of time over and to spare with which I could make satisfaction for my misspent past. I have only those times which are coming to work on. And what is more, I know very well that because of my appalling weakness and dull-wittedness I should only be able to heed one impulse in a hundred. What a plight I am in! Help me, now, for the love of Jesus!'

How right you are to say 'for the love of Jesus'. For it is in the love of Jesus that you have your help. The nature of love is such that it shares everything. Love Jesus, and everything he has is yours. Because he is God, he is maker and giver of time. Because he is Man, he has given true heed to time. Because he is both God and Man he is the best judge of the spending of time. Unite yourself to him by love and trust, and by that union you will be joined both to him and to all who like yourself are united by love to him . . . with our lady, St Mary, who, full of grace, perfectly heeded every passing moment; with all the angels in heaven, who have never let time pass; and with all the saints in heaven and on earth, who by their love, and by Jesus' grace, take proper account of every moment.

This is a great comfort. Really understand it, and get profit therefrom. But let me emphasize this: I cannot see that anyone can claim fellowship in this matter with Jesus or his righteous Mother, his angels or his saints, unless he is doing everything in his power, with the help of grace, to attend to each moment of time . . . so that he can be seen to be doing his part to strengthen the fellowship, however little it may be, as each of them, in his turn, is doing his.

So pay great attention to this marvellous work of grace within your soul. It is always a sudden impulse and comes without warning, springing up to God like some spark from the fire. An incredible number of such impulses arise in one brief hour in the soul who has a will to this work! In one such flash the soul may completely forget the created world outside. Yet almost as quickly it may relapse back to thoughts and memories of things done and undone – all because of our fallen nature. And as fast again it may rekindle.

This then, in brief, is how it works. It is obviously not make-believe, nor wrong thinking, nor fanciful opinion. These would not be the product of a devout and humble love, but the outcome of the pride and inventiveness of the imagination. If this work of grace is to be truly and genuinely understood, all such proud imaginings must ruthlessly be stamped out!

For whoever hears or reads about all this, and thinks that it is fundamentally an activity of the mind, and proceeds then to work it all out along these lines, is on quite the wrong track. He manufactures an experience that is neither spiritual nor physical. He is dangerously misled and in real peril. So much so, that unless God in his great goodness intervenes with a miracle of mercy and makes him stop and submit to the advice of those who really know, he will go mad, or suffer some other dreadful form of spiritual mischief and devilish deceit. Indeed, almost casually as it were, he may be lost eternally, body and soul. So for the love of God be careful, and do not attempt to achieve this experience intellectually. I tell you truly it cannot come this way. So leave it alone.

Do not think that because I call it a 'darkness' or a 'cloud' it is the sort of cloud you see in the sky, or the kind of darkness you know at home when the light is out. That kind of darkness or cloud you can picture in your mind's eye in the height of summer, just as in the depth of a winter's night you can picture a clear and shining light. I do not mean this at all. By 'darkness' I mean 'a lack of knowing' – just as anything that you do not know or may have forgotten may be said to be 'dark' to you, for you cannot see it with your inward eye. For this reason it is called 'a cloud', not of the sky, of course, but 'of unknowing', a cloud of unknowing between you and your God.

5 IF ever you are to come to this cloud and live and work in it, as I suggest, then just as this cloud of unknowing is as it were above you, between you and God, so you must also put a cloud of forgetting beneath you and all creation. We are apt to think that we are very far from God because of this cloud of unknowing between us and him, but surely it would be more correct to say that we are much farther from him if there is no cloud of forgetting between us and the whole created world. Whenever I say 'the whole created world' I always mean not only the individual

creatures therein, but everything connected with them. There is no exception whatever, whether you think of them as physical or spiritual beings, or of their states or actions, or of their goodness or badness. In a word, everything must be hidden under this cloud of forgetting.

For though it is sometimes helpful to think of particular creatures, what they are and do, in this case it is virtually useless. For the act of remembering or thinking about what a thing is or does has a spiritual effect. Your soul's eye concentrates upon it, just as the marksman fixes his eye on his target. Let me say this: everything you think about, all the time you think about it, is 'above' you, between you and God. And you are that much farther from God if anything but God is in your mind.

Indeed, if we may say so reverently, when we are engaged on this work it profits little or nothing to think even of God's kindness or worth, or of our Lady, or of the saints or angels, or of the joys of heaven, if you think thereby by such meditation to strengthen your purpose. In this particular matter it will help not at all. For though it is good to think about the kindness of God, and to love him and praise him for it, it is far better to think about him as he is, and to love and praise him for himself.

Think of God NOT in terms of his creation

6 BUT now you will ask me, 'How am I to think of God himself, and what is he?' and I cannot answer you except to say 'I do not know!' For with this question you have brought me into the same darkness, the same cloud of unknowing where I want you to be! For though we through the grace of God can know fully about all other matters, and think about them – yes, even the very works of God himself – yet of God himself can no man think.

Therefore I will leave on one side everything I can think, and choose for my love that thing which I cannot think! Why? Because he may well be loved, but not thought. By love he can be caught and held, but by thinking never. Therefore, though it may be good sometimes to think particularly about God's kindness and worth, and though it may be enlightening too, and a part of contemplation, yet in the work now before us it must be put down and covered with a cloud of forgetting. And you are to step over it resolutely and eagerly, with a devout and kindling love, and try to penetrate that darkness above you. Strike that thick cloud of unknowing with the sharp dart of longing love, and on no account whatever think of giving up.

7 SHOULD any thought arise and obtrude itself between you and the darkness, asking what you are seeking, and what you are wanting, answer that it is God you want: 'Him I covet, him I seek, and nothing but him.'

Should he (the thought) ask, 'What is this God?' answer that it is the God who made you and redeemed you, and who has, through his grace, called you to his love. 'And', tell him, 'you do not even know the first thing about him.' And then go on to say, 'Get down', and proceed to trample on him out of love for God; yes, even when such thoughts seem to be holy, and calculated to help you find God. Quite possibly he will bring to your mind many lovely and wonderful thoughts of his kindness, and remind you of God's sweetness and love, his grace and mercy. If you will but listen to him, he asks no more. He will go on chattering increasingly, and bring you steadily down to think of Christ's Passion. There he will show you the wonderful kindness of God, and he wants nothing so much as that you should listen to him. For he will then go on to let you see your past manner of life, and as you think of its wretchedness your mind will be well away, back in its old haunts. Before you know where you are you are disintegrated beyond belief! And the reason? Simply that you freely consented to listen to that thought, and responded to it, accepted it, and gave it its head.

And yet of course the thought was both good and holy, and indeed necessary, so that, paradoxically, no man or woman can hope to achieve contemplation without the foundation of many such delightful meditations on his or her own wretchedness, and our Lord's Passion, and the kindness of God, and his great goodness and worth. All the same, the practised hand must leave them, and put them away deep down in the cloud of forgetting if he is ever to penetrate the cloud of unknowing between him and God.

So when you feel by the grace of God that he is calling you to this work, and you intend to respond, lift your heart to God with humble love. And really mean God himself who created you, and bought you, and graciously called you to this state of life. And think no other thought of him. It all depends on your desire. A naked intention directed to God, and himself alone, is wholly sufficient.

If you want this intention summed up in a word, to retain it more easily, take a short word, preferably of one syllable, to do so. The shorter the word the better, being more like the working of the Spirit. A word like 'GOD' or 'LOVE'. Choose which you like, or perhaps some other, so long as it is of one syllable. And fix this word fast to your heart, so that it is always there come what may. It will be your shield and spear in peace and war alike. With this word you will hammer the cloud and the darkness above you. With this word you will suppress all thought under the cloud of forgetting. So much so that if ever you are tempted to think what it is that you are seeking, this one word will be sufficient answer. And if you would go on to think learnedly about the significance and analysis of that same word, tell yourself that you will have it whole, and not in bits and pieces. If you hold fast, that thought will surely go. And why? Because you refuse to let it feed on the helpful meditations we spoke of earlier.

8 BUT naturally you will ask whether it is a good thing or an evil which keeps obtruding itself into your thoughts. 'If it were evil', you would say, 'I am surprised that it increases a man's devotion so greatly. Sometimes, as I know very well, it is most inspiring to heed such thoughts. Sometimes they move me to heartfelt tears and pity for the passion of Christ, or for my own wretchedness; and sometimes for other reasons that seem both holy and helpful. I think therefore that such thoughts cannot really be evil. And if they are so good and helpful it is very strange indeed that you should bid me put them away under this cloud of forgetting.'

I agree that it is a very good point, and I will try to answer it as well as I can, however inadequately. In the first place if you are to ask me what it is that thrusts itself upon you and offers its help, I answer that it is manifestly the expression of your normal mind, the reasoning power of your soul, Again, if you ask whether it is good or evil, I say that fundamentally it must always be good, for reason is a godlike thing. But the use we make of it be either good or evil. It is good when, by grace, you see your own wretchedness. or behold the passion of our Lord, or the kindness and wonderful works of God in his creation, physical and spiritual. Then, as you say, it is not strange that it should greatly foster devotion. But reason becomes evil when pride inflates it, or much learning and book knowledge – as in some clergy, for example! It makes them anxious to be known not for their skill in things divine and devout, but as proud Scholars – of the devil! – and Masters – of vanity and lies! In all men and women, religious or secular, normal reason becomes evil when it makes them proud of their worldly attainments; when they covet position, possessions, pomps, and popularity in this present world.

Were you to ask why you should suppress all this in the cloud of forgetting, since it is basically good, and when used well, so profitable and helpful, my reply would be to tell you that there are two ways of life in Holy Church. One is the active, the other is the contemplative life. Active is the lower, contemplative the higher. The active life has two parts, a higher and a lower, and likewise the contemplative has two parts too, a lower and a higher. These two ways of life are linked, and though they are different, each is dependent on the other. For what we call the higher part of the active life is the same as the lower part of the contemplative. A man cannot be fully active except he be partly contemplative, nor fully contemplative (at least on earth) without being partly active. Active life is begun and ended in this life; not so the contemplative. It begins in this life and goes on eternally. The part that Mary chose 'shall not be taken away'.[1] Active life is 'careful and troubled about many things'; contemplative sits peacefully with one.

The lower part of the active life consists of good, straightforward acts of mercy and charity. The higher part (which is the lower part of contemplative living) is made

1. Luke 10: 42 (The footnotes throughout are the translator's.)

up of various things, for example, spiritual meditation, an awareness of one's own wretched state, sorrow and contrition, a sympathetic and understanding consideration of Christ's passion and that of his servants, a gratitude which praises God for his wonderful gifts, his kindness and works in all parts of his creation, physical and spiritual. But the higher part of contemplation – at least as we know it in this life – is wholly caught up in darkness, and in this cloud of unknowing, with an outreaching love and a blind groping for the naked being of God, himself and him only.

Everything a man does in the lower part of active life is necessarily exterior to him, so to speak, beneath him. In the higher part (the lower part of the contemplative) a man's activity is inward, within himself, and he is, so to speak, on the level. In the higher part of the contemplative life a man is definitely reaching above himself and is inferior to none but God. Above himself undoubtedly, because his deliberate intention is to win by grace what he cannot attain by nature, namely, to be united to God in spirit, one with him in love and will.

Just as it is impossible (from our point of view) for a man to practise the higher part of the active life without temporarily ceasing from the lower part, so a man cannot come to the higher part of the contemplative without ceasing from the lower. Similarly, just as it would be an improper thing, and a handicap, for a man engaged in meditation to consider his 'exterior works' – what he had done or ought to do, however holy those works might be – so surely it is just as much improper and a handicap for a man who ought to be working in divine darkness, and in this cloud of unknowing, whose love is moving out to God himself, to allow any thought or meditation of God's wonderful gifts, or kindness, or any of his created works, physical or spiritual, to obtrude itself between him and his

God – however pleasant or inspiring those thoughts may be.

It is for this reason that I say you are to suppress these insidious thoughts, and cover them up with a thick cloud of forgetting, even when they are holy and promise well to achieve your object. Why, love may reach up to God himself even in this life – but not knowledge. All the while the soul dwells in this corruptible body, the clarity of our spiritual understanding, especially of God, is touched with some sort of distortion, which causes our works to be imperfect, and which, apart from God's wonderful grace, would be fruitful of much error.

9 THEREFORE the vigorous working of your imagination, which is always so active when you set yourself to this blind contemplation, must as often be suppressed. Unless you suppress it, it will suppress you! Often enough when you are thinking that you are abiding in this darkness and there is only God in your mind, if you look carefully you will find your mind not occupied with this darkness at all, but definitely engaged with something less than God. And if this is so, then that thing can be said to be temporarily on top of you, and between you and God. Make up your mind, therefore, to put down all such reflections, holy and attractive though they be. I tell you this: it is more profitable to your soul's health, more worthwhile, more pleasing to God and the hosts of Heaven – yes, more helpful to your friends, natural and spiritual, dead or alive – that you should have this blind outreaching love to God himself, this secret love pressing upon the cloud of unknowing, that you should have this as your spiritual affection, than that you should contemplate and gaze on the angels and saints in heaven, and hear the happy music of the blessed.

73

Do not be surprised at this. See it once (and by grace you can), get hold of it and feel it, and you will see it always. Be quite sure that you will never have the unclouded vision of God here in this life. But you may have the awareness of him, if he is willing by his grace to give it you. So lift up your love to that cloud. Or, more accurately, let God draw your love up to that cloud. And strive by his grace to forget all else.

For if the bare thought of anything at all, rising unbidden in your mind, serves to remove you further from God than you would otherwise be (it gets in your way and renders you less able to experience his love), how much more frustrating will be the thought that is deliberately entertained and sustained? And if this is true when you think about saints or any suitable spiritual object, how much more will you be hindered when you consider ordinary mortals in this wretched life, or other physical or worldly things?

I am not saying that the spontaneous, unexpected thought of any good and spiritual thing which demands the attention of your mind and will, or a thought that you have deliberately conjured up to strengthen your devotion, is therefore evil, even though it is a hindrance. God forbid that you should so understand me. But I do say that for all its goodness and holiness, all the while a man seeks to contemplate, it is more of a hindrance than a help. Surely he who seeks God perfectly will not rest finally in the recollection of any angel or saint in heaven.

10 BUT it is not so with any and every recollection of any living person or thing. For a spontaneous thought, springing to mind unsought and unwittingly, cannot be

reckoned to be sin. It may be sin, if you like, in the sense that it is the result of original sin, depriving you of power over all your thoughts – you were cleansed from the guilt of that when you were baptized. It can only become sin if this sudden impulse is not quickly put down, because immediately your natural attention will be attracted by it. It may be something you like, a thing that pleases you, or has pleased you in the past, or it may be a grouse over something that grieves you, or has grieved you. To a man or woman already living in mortal sin, this attention may be mortally sinful; but to you, and all others who have honestly forsaken the world and live devoutly under obedience to Holy Church (privately or publicly is immaterial), intending to be ruled not by your own will or knowledge, but by that of your superiors, religious or secular, neither this natural liking nor grumbling is more than venial sin. The reason is that your intention was rooted and grounded in God when you first entered that state in which you now stand with the knowledge and direction of some discreet father.

But if you allow houseroom to this thing that you naturally like or grouse about, and make no attempt to rebuke it, ultimately it will take root in your inmost being, in your will, and with the consent of your will. Then it is deadly sin. This happens whenever you, or any of those I have been speaking of, deliberately conjure up the memory of somebody or something or other. If it is a thing that grieves or has grieved you, then you rage and want revenge – and that is *Wrath*. Or you will despise and loathe it, and think spitefully and harshly of it – and that is *Envy*. Or you will get weary and bored with being good in spirit and body – and that is *Sloth*.

And if it is a pleasant thing, present or past, you experience a passing delight when you think about it, whatever

75

it may be. So that you dwell on it, and in the end fix your heart and will on it, and turn to it for nourishment. You think, at such times, that you want never better than to live in peace and quiet with this pleasant thing. Now, if this thought that you deliberately conjure up, or harbour, and dwell lovingly upon, is natural worth or knowledge, charm or station, favour or beauty – then it is *Pride*. If it is a matter of worldly goods, riches, or possessions, ownership or lordship, then it is *Avarice*. If it is a matter of choice food and drink, or any other delight of the palate, then it is *Gluttony*. If it is love or pleasure, or flirting, fawning, and flattering, for another or for yourself – then it is *Lust*.

[margin handwriting: sin]

11 I AM not saying this because I believe you or anyone else I have been speaking about to be guilty of and hampered by such sins, but because I want you to weigh up carefully every such thought and impulse, and to work hard at destroying it as soon as it makes it appearance with its opportunity for you to sin. For I tell you this: whoever does not weigh up, or who sets little store by, first thoughts, even if to him they are not sinful, shall not avoid rashness in venial sin. No man can utterly avoid venial sin in this mortal life. But recklessness in venial sin ought always to be avoided by all true disciples of perfection. If not, then no wonder they soon go on to mortal sin!

[margin handwriting: take control over your sin]

12 So if you are to stand and not fall, never give up your firm intention: beat away at this cloud of unknowing between you and God with that sharp dart of longing love. Hate to think about anything less than God, and let nothing

whatever distract you from this purpose. It is only thus that you can destroy the ground and root of sin.

Were you to fast beyond all measure, or watch at great length, or rise at the crack of dawn, or sleep on boards and wear chains – yes, if it were lawful (and it is not!) for you to pluck out your eyes, cut out your tongue, stop your ears and nose, amputate your limbs, and afflict your body with all the pain you could possibly think of – this would not help you at all. The urge and impulse of sin would still be with you.

More: however much you might weep in sorrow for your sins, or for the sufferings of Christ, or however much you might think of the delights of heaven, what good would it do you? Much good, surely; much help; much profit; much grace. But compared with this blind out-reaching of love . . . there is very little indeed that it can do without love. This, in itself, is the 'best part' that Mary chose.[1] Without it all the rest is virtually worthless. Negatively, it destroys the ground and root of sin, and positively it acquires virtue. For if this love is there in truth, so too will all other virtues truly, perfectly, and knowingly, be included in it. And the firm intention will be unaffected. Without it a man may have as many virtues as he likes; every one of them will be tainted and warped, and to that extent imperfect.

For virtue is nothing but an ordered, deliberate affection, plainly directed to God, for his own sake. How? God in himself is the pure cause of all virtues. If anyone should be moved to seek a particular virtue from mixed motives, even if God were his chief reason, such a virtue would be imperfect. We shall see this if we select a virtue or two as examples. These two virtues might well be love and humility. For whoever has clearly got these needs no more: he has all.

1. Luke 10: 42.

13 LET us take a look first of all at humility. We shall see that it is 'imperfect' when it springs from mixed motives, even if God be its chief reason; and that it is 'perfect' when it is caused solely by God. In the first place we must know what humility is if we are to understand it properly: then we may be able to assess more truly what is its cause. In itself, humility is nothing else but a true knowledge and awareness of oneself as one really is. For surely whoever truly saw and felt himself as he is, would truly be humble. Two things cause humility. One is the degradation, wretchedness, and weakness of man to which by sin he has fallen: he ought to be aware of this, partially at any rate, all the time he lives, however holy he may be. The other is the superabundant love and worth of God in himself: gazing on which all nature trembles, all scholars are fools, all saints and angels blind. So much so that had he not, in his divine wisdom, measured their vision of himself according to their progress in grace, words would fail to say what would happen to them.

This latter cause is the 'perfect' one; it is eternal. The former is 'imperfect': not only is it temporal, but often as not a soul in this mortal body, because the grace of God increases his longing (as often and for as long as God wishes), suddenly becomes completely oblivious of himself, not worrying if he is wretched or holy. Whether or not this happens often or seldom to the prepared soul, it never lasts more than a short while. In this time it is perfectly humble, for then it knows no cause but the chief, which is God himself. But when it knows and is moved by the other cause, even if God himself is the chief motive, its humility is still imperfect. All the same it is good, and should be experienced. God forbid that you should misunderstand me.

14 FOR though I call it 'imperfect' humility, I would much rather have a real knowledge and awareness of myself as I am in this way than be without it. And I fancy it would bring me sooner to 'perfect' humility itself, its cause and its virtue, than would be the case if the whole company of heaven, saints and angels, with Holy Church on earth, men and women, religious and secular, in their different states, were to band together for this one thing, to pray God that I might get perfect humility! Yes, it is impossible for a sinner to get or keep perfect humility without it.

Therefore strain every nerve in every possible way to know and experience yourself as you really are. It will not be long, I suspect, before you have a real knowledge and experience of God as he is. Not as he is in himself, of course, for that is impossible to any save God; and not as you will in Heaven, both in body and soul. But as much as is now possible for a humble soul in a mortal body to know and experience him . . . and as much as he will permit.

Now do not go thinking that, because I say there are two causes of humility, I want you to give up the hard work of 'imperfect' humility and to concentrate wholly on the 'perfect'. Indeed not. You will never acquire it like that. But I am doing what I am because I want to tell you and to let you see how much more worth-while this spiritual exercise is than any other physical or spiritual work, even when this is done under the inspiration of grace. How that the secret love of a purified soul, continually pressing into this dark cloud of unknowing between you and God, truly and perfectly contains within itself that perfect humility, seeking as it does nothing less than God. And, too, because I want you to know what perfect humility consists of, and to set it up for your heart to love, for your sake and mine.

And because I want, by this knowledge, to make you humbler still.

I think that the want of knowledge often is the cause of much pride! For probably, if you did not know what perfect humility was, you would think that when you had had a little knowledge and experience of what I call imperfect humility you had almost attained the perfect variety. So you would deceive yourself into thinking you were completely humble when all the time you were eaten up with abominable pride! Therefore, try your very hardest to come by perfect humility. Its nature is such that he who has it, all the time he has it, simply does not sin. And not very much afterwards, when it has passed.

15 You must believe me when I say that there is this perfect humility and that we can attain it, by God's grace, in this life. I say this to refute the error which claims that perfect humility is caused by the remembrance of our wretchedness and past sins. I readily grant that for habitual sinners like myself it is both essential and effective to be humbled by the recollection of one's wretchedness and past sins; and to be humbled until such time as the deterioration of sin be made good both in our consciences and in our minds. But to comparative innocents, who have never sinned mortally, habitually or deliberately, but only through weakness and ignorance, and who are set on becoming contemplatives – and to us too, if our director and our conscience testify that we have truly amended through contrition, confession and penance, according to the rules of All-holy Church, and more especially if we feel moved by grace to become contemplatives – there is another cause which will humble them. This cause is as far above the

imperfect cause as the manner of life of our Lady St Mary is above that of the most sinful penitent in Holy Church, or as the life of Christ is above that of any other man, or as the life of an angel, who has never known, or will know, human weakness, is above that of the weakest man on earth.

If there were no perfect cause to make one humble, but only the knowledge of our own wretchedness, I should like to ask those who hold this view what it is that humbles those who do not know, and will never know, the wretchedness of sin. I mean our Lord Jesus Christ, our Lady St Mary, and all the saints and angels in heaven. That we should be perfect in this as in all things, our Lord Jesus Christ himself calls us in the Gospel, when he bids us be perfect by grace, as he is by nature.[1]

16 No one need think he presumes because he, the most wretched sinner in the world, now dares, after true amendment and a subsequent call to contemplation, and with the full approval of his director and his conscience, to offer God his humble love, and secretly to press into that cloud of unknowing between him and God. For our Lord said to Mary Magdalene, the typical representative of sinners called to the contemplative life, 'Thy sins be forgiven thee.'[2] Not for her great sorrow; not for her anxiety over her sins; not for her humility as she contemplated her wretchedness; but, surely, because she loved much.

This is the point where we can see what secret and urgent love may obtain from our Lord; far beyond anything we could do or imagine. I grant that she was deeply penitent, and shed bitter tears over her sins, and was greatly humbled

1. Matthew 5: 48.   2. Luke 7: 47.

at the thought of her own wretchedness. We, likewise, who are wretched and habitual sinners, should all our lifetime be penitent, fearful, and aweful, humbled to the full as we recall our wretchedness.

But how? In the same way as Mary, surely. Though she might not always feel deeply sorry for her sins, all her life she would carry the burden of them in her heart and memory. But as the Bible shows her sorrow was more heartfelt, her longing more grievous, her sighing more profound, her languishing indeed nearly fatal, because she wanted to love God more. It was this, far more than the recollection of her sins. And this, even when she was already loving much. We need not be surprised; it is characteristic of the true lover that the more he loves, the more he wants to love.

Yet she was quite clear in her own mind that she was the most appalling of all sinners, and that her sins had made the gulf between her and the God she loved so much, and that they were the major cause that she was weak, and wanted to love God, and did not. What of it? Did she descend from the heights of her longing to the deeps of her sinful life to search in the filth and sewage of her sins, fetching them up one by one, brooding and sorrowing and weeping over each in turn? Of course she didn't! Why? Because God let her know, by his grace in her soul, that she could never bring it about this way. It was far more likely that she would begin to sin again if she had done this, than that she should thereby gain forgiveness for those sins.

Therefore she has pinned her love and her longing desire to this cloud of unknowing, and has learned to love what in this life certainly she will never clearly understand with her mind, nor delight in with her emotions. And she so loves that often as not she forgets that she has been a sinner herself. Yes, and I think that for the most part she is--so engrossed in loving his Godhead that she gives little thought to the beauty and loveliness of his physical body, while he sits and speaks to her, precious and blessed though it is – nor, for that matter, to anything else, physical or spiritual. This seems to be the Gospel's teaching on this point.

17 ST LUKE tells us that when our Lord was in the house of Martha her sister, all the time that Martha was busying herself preparing his meal, Mary sat at his feet. And as she listened to him she regarded neither her sister's busy-ness (and it was a good and holy business; is it not the first part of the active life?) nor his priceless and blessed physical perfection, nor the beauty of his human voice and words (and this is an advance, for this is the second part of the active life, as well as the first part of the contemplative). But what she was looking at was the supreme wisdom of his Godhead shrouded by the words of his humanity.

And on this she gazed with all the love of her heart. Nothing she saw or heard could budge her, but there she sat, completely still, with deep delight, and an urgent love eagerly reaching out into that high cloud of unknowing that was between her and God.

I want to say this: no one in this life, however pure, and however enraptured with contemplating and loving God, is ever without this intervening, high, and wonderful cloud. It was in this same cloud that Mary experienced the many secret movements of her love. Why? Because this is the highest and holiest state of contemplation we can know on earth.

From 'this part'[1] nothing on earth could move her. So much so, that when her sister Martha complained to our

1. Luke 10:42.

Lord, and told him to tell her to get up and help her, and not leave her to do all the work by herself, Mary sat completely still and silent, showing not the least indication of any grumble or complaint she herself might have against her sister. It is not surprising: she had other work to do that Martha did not understand, and she had no time to spare for her, or for answering her complaint.

My friend, all that took place between our Lord and these two sisters – these works and words and behaviour– are meant for an example for all the actives and contemplatives that have since arisen in Holy Church – and shall be till the Day of Judgement. Mary is the type of contemplatives, that they should match their lives with hers, and in the same sort of way Martha stands for the actives.

18 JUST as then Martha complained of Mary her sister, so to this day do actives complain of contemplatives. Wherever you find anyone, man or woman, in any body of people, religious or secular (there are no exceptions), who feels moved through God's grace and guidance to forsake all outward activity and set about living the contemplative life and who, as I say, knows what he is about, his conscience and advisers corroborating, just as soon will you find his brothers, sisters, best friends, and sundry others, who know nothing of his inward urge, or the contemplative life itself, rise up with great complaint, and sharply reprove him, and tell him he is wasting his time. And they will recount all sorts of tales, some false and some true, describing how men and women who have given themselves up to such a life in the past have fallen. There is never a tale of those who make good.

Many do fall, and have fallen, who have seemingly

forsaken the world – I grant all that. And when they should have become God's servants and his contemplatives, because they would not rule themselves by true and spiritual teaching, they have become the devil's servants and his contemplatives, and are now hypocrites or heretics or fanatics and so forth, to the detriment of Holy Church. I am not going to speak about this now, for we would digress too far. Later on, perhaps, if God wills and it is necessary, we may look at something of their state, and the reason why they fell. But now no more: we must press on.

19 It might be thought that I am paying scant respect to Martha, that special saint, in comparing her complaints with those of worldly men, or theirs with hers. I can truthfully say I mean no dishonour to her or to them. God forbid that I should say anything derogatory of any of God's servants of whatever degree, and particularly of this, his special saint. I think we can understand and excuse her complaint when we consider the circumstances, both of time and manner. She spoke without knowledge. It is not surprising that she did not know at the time how Mary was occupied, for I very much doubt if she had previously heard much about such perfection. Too, what she said she said courteously and succinctly. We must hold her completely exonerated!

In the same way I think these men and women of the world must quite definitely be excused for the complaints already mentioned, however rude they may have been. They, too, were ignorant. Just as Martha, when she made her complaint, knew very little of what Mary was doing, these people nowadays similarly know little or nothing of what young disciples of God mean when they withdraw from the business of the world, and are led to be God's special servants, both because they are to be holy, and because it is spiritually right for them. If they did know, I am quite sure they would not act or speak as they do. I think, therefore, that we have got to consider them excused: they have no idea of any kind of life better than their own! Moreover, when I think of my own past countless faults of word and deed, committed through ignorance, I recall at the same time that if I am to be excused by God for these sins of ignorance, I must also in common charity and mercy excuse other men's ignorant words and deeds – always. Otherwise, surely, I am not doing to others as I would they should do to me.

20 I THINK, therefore, that they who set out to be contemplatives should not only excuse actives when they complain, but should themselves be so spiritually occupied that they pay little or no attention to what men say or do to them. Mary, who is our example in all this, did this when her sister Martha complained to our Lord, and if we will do the same, our Lord will do for us today what he did then for Mary.

And what was that? Surely this: our loving Lord Jesus Christ, from whom no secrets are hidden, when Martha demanded that he should act as judge and tell Mary to get up and help her serve him, because he saw that Mary's spirit was ardently loving his Godhead, with great courtesy and propriety himself answered for her. She would not leave her love for him in order to answer for herself. How did he answer? Certainly not as the judge to whom Martha appealed, but as an advocate he lawfully defended her who loved him, and said 'Martha, Martha!'[1] He named her name twice for her good, for he wanted her to listen and attend to his words. 'Thou art very busy,' he said, 'and troubled about many things.' (Actives have to be busy and concerned about a whole variety of matters to provide for their own needs, and for their deeds of mercy to fellow Christians, as Christian charity requires.) He said this to Martha because he wanted her to know that what she was doing was good and useful to her spiritual health. But in order that she might not think that what she was doing was the highest and best that man could do, he added, 'But one thing is necessary.'

What is that one thing? Surely that God is loved and praised for himself alone, above all else that a man can do, physically or spiritually. And to stop Martha thinking that she could love and praise God above all else whatsoever, and still be busied in the affairs of this life, and to settle her question whether or not she could serve God in a physical way and a spiritual at the same time – she could do it imperfectly, but not perfectly – he added that Mary had 'chosen the best part, which should never be taken from her.' For that perfect outreaching of love which begins here on earth is the same as that which shall last eternally in the blessedness of heaven; it is all one.

21 WHAT does this mean, 'Mary hath chosen the best'? Whenever we speak of 'best' we postulate the existence of a 'good' and 'a better' so that 'the best' is a third thing. What are these three good things of which Mary chose 'the best'? Not three lives, for Holy Church only knows of two, the active and contemplative; which two

1. Luke 10:41.

lives are illustrated for us in the Gospel by the two sisters, Martha and Mary. Martha represents the active life, Mary the contemplative. Without one of these lives no man can be saved, yet when there is no more than two no man can choose 'the best'.

But though there are only two lives, these two lives have between them three parts, each one better than the other. These three have been already mentioned earlier in the book, in their correct order. As we said there, the first part consists of the good and honest physical works of mercy and charity. This is the first stage of the active life, as we have already said. The second part of these two lives consists of good spiritual meditations on our own wretchedness, on the sufferings of Christ, and on the joy of heaven. The first part is good: the second is better, for it is the second stage of the active life and the first of the contemplative. In this part the contemplative and active lives are knit together in a spiritual relationship, and made sisters like Martha and Mary. To such a height of contemplation may an active come, yet no higher except on the rarest occasions, and then by special grace: to such a depth may a contemplative descend towards the active life, but no lower, except on the rarest occasions, and in times of great need.

The third part of these two lives is caught up in this dark cloud of unknowing, and has many a secret act of love to God as he is. The first part is good, and second better, the third best of all. And this is Mary's 'best part'. It is plain why our Lord did not say to Martha that Mary hath chosen the best 'life' for there are only two lives, and no one can choose the best of two. But of these two lives he said 'Mary hath chosen the best part, which shall never be taken from her.' Although the first and second parts are both good and holy, yet they end with this life. In the life to

come there will be no need for works of mercy, or to weep
for our wretchedness or for the Passion of Christ. For then
shall no one hunger or thirst, as he may do today, or die of
cold, be ill, homeless, or in prison – nor even need burying,
for no one will die.

The third part that Mary chose, let that man choose who
is called by God's grace to choose. Or, if I may put it more
truly, whoever is chosen by God for that part, let him set
about it with vigour and joy. For that part shall never be
taken away. It begins here, but it goes on for ever.

Let our Lord cry to these actives as if he now were speaking to them on our behalf as he did once to Martha for
Mary, 'Martha, Martha!' 'Actives, Actives! be as busy as
you can in the first two parts, now in one, now in the other,
and if you really want to, in both courageously. But don't
interfere with my contemplatives. You don't know what is
happening to them. Leave them to their "sitting" and "resting" and enjoyment, with the third and best part of Mary.'

22 SWEET indeed was that love between our Lord
and Mary. Much love had she for him. Much more had he
for her. Whoever would really understand what passed
between him and her – not superficially, but as the Gospel
story, which is never wrong, testifies – would find that her
love for him was so heartfelt, that nothing less than himself
could satisfy her, nor keep her heart from him. This is the
same Mary who, when she sought him at the sepulchre,
weeping, would not be comforted by angels.[1] For when
they spoke to her so gently and lovingly, 'Weep not, Mary;
our Lord whom thou seekest is risen, and thou shalt have
him, and see him alive in all his beauty among his disciples

1. John 20:11–13.

in Galilee, as he said', she would not stop weeping for them. Because she thought that whoever was seeking the King of angels would not stop for mere angels.

What else? Surely everyone who looks carefully into the Gospel story will find many other wonderful cases of her perfect love written for our example so closely in harmony with the teaching in this book that they might have been set down for that very purpose! And, indeed, so they were, whatever one may say. If a man is prepared to see there in the Gospel the wonderful and especial love our Lord had for her, the type of every habitual sinner truly converted and called to the grace of contemplation, he will find that our Lord will not allow anyone, not even her own sister, to speak a word against her, but will defend her himself. More: he rebuked Simon the leper in his own home, because he criticized her mentally.[1] This is great love; indeed, surpassing love.

23 UNDOUBTEDLY, if we will earnestly conform our love and our manner of living to that of Mary as best we can, helped by grace and direction, our Lord will spiritually answer for us today in the inmost hearts of all who criticize us. I am not going to say that we shall never have our detractors or critics all the while we struggle on, any more than Mary did. But I am prepared to say that, if we give no more heed to their criticisms than did she, and do not give up our interior, spiritual efforts either, then our Lord will answer them in spirit (that is, if they are sincere in their criticisms) in such a way that they will very soon be ashamed of their words and thoughts.

And as he will answer for us in men's hearts, so will he

1. Luke 7: 44.

also move others to give us the necessities of life, food and clothing and so forth, if he sees that we are not going to give up loving him to attend to such matters. I say this to refute the error which claims that it is wrong to serve God in the contemplative life unless one has secured adequate provision beforehand. They say that 'God helps them that help themselves'. But, in fact, they malign him, as they well know. For you can be absolutely confident of this, whoever you are that has truly left the world for God, that God will send you one of two things, independently of your own efforts: either an abundant supply of goods, or else the physical strength and spiritual patience to endure want. So what does it matter which a man has? It is all one to the true contemplative. Whoever doubts this, either the devil of hell is in his heart depriving him of faith, or else he is not so truly converted as he should be, however clever he may be, and whatever pious excuses he may produce.

Therefore, you who set out to be a contemplative as Mary was, choose rather to be humbled by the unimaginable greatness and incomparable perfection of God than by your own wretchedness and imperfection. In other words, look more to God's worthiness than to your own worthlessness. To the perfectly humble there is nothing lacking, spiritual or physical. For they have God, in whom is all abundance, and whoever has him – as this book keeps on saying – needs nothing else in this life.

24 WE said of humility that it was mysteriously and perfectly summed up in this little, blind loving of God, beating away at this dark cloud of unknowing, all else buried and forgotten. We may say this, however, of all the virtues, and in particular of charity. For charity is nothing

else than loving God for himself, above all created things, and loving men in God just as we love ourselves. It is quite right that in contemplation God should be loved for himself alone above all created things, for as we have said already, this work is fundamentally a naked intent, none other than the single-minded intention of our spirit directed to God himself alone.

I call it 'single-minded' because in this matter the perfect apprentice asks neither to be spared pain, nor to be generously rewarded, nor indeed for anything but God himself. So that he cares not whether he be grieved or glad, but only that the will of him whom he loves be fulfilled. And so it is that God is perfectly loved for himself, and above all his creation. For in this work a contemplative will not permit the least thought of the very holiest thing to share his attention. As he does this, he fulfils the second, lower branch of charity (which is love to his fellow Christian) truly and perfectly, as you can prove. For the perfect contemplative holds no man as such in special regard, be he kinsman, stranger, friend, or foe. For all men alike are his brothers, and none strangers. He considers all men his friends, and none his foes. To such an extent that even those who hurt and injure him he reckons to be real and special friends, and he is moved to wish for them as much good as he would wish for his very dearest friend.

25 YOU will notice that I do not say that in this work he should have a special regard for any man on earth, friend or foe, relative or stranger. For this cannot happen in perfect contemplation when everything less than God is completely forgotten, as it ought to be.

But what I am saying is that he will be made so virtuous

and charitable through contemplation, that ever afterwards when he comes down from the heights to talk with or pray for his fellow Christians, his will will be as readily directed to his foes as to his friends, to strangers as to relatives.

Yes, and sometimes more to foes than to friends!

Not that he ought to come away from his occupation with God, for that would be great sin. But sometimes, of course, he has to descend from the heights, quickly and necessarily at the behest of charity.

Nevertheless, in this work of loving God, he has no time to consider who is friend or foe, brother or stranger. I do not say that he will not feel at times – indeed, quite often – deeper affection for some than for others. This is only right, and for many reasons. Love asks just that. For Christ felt a deeper affection for John, and Mary, and Peter, than for many others. But when the soul is wholly turned to God all people are equally dear to him, for he then feels no other cause for loving than God himself. So all are loved simply and sincerely, for God's sake as well as his own.

For as all men are lost in Adam, and show by their works their desire for salvation, and are saved by reason of the sufferings of Christ and none other, so, as experience goes to show, and in a not dissimilar way, a soul that is wholly given to contemplation, and therefore one with God in spirit, does everything it can to make all men as whole as itself. When a limb of our body aches, all the other limbs suffer in sympathy, and when a limb is sound, the others rejoice with it. It is precisely the same spiritually with the limbs of Holy Church. Christ is our head, we his limbs, if we abide in charity, and he who would be our Lord's perfect disciple must strain every nerve and muscle of his soul in this spiritual work to save his earthly brothers and sisters, just as our Lord did with his body on the Cross. How does he do this? Not only for his friends, his nearest and dearest, but by and large for all mankind, without more attention to one than to another. For all who will quit sin and ask God's mercy will be saved by reason of Christ's sufferings.

As it is with humility and charity, so it works out with all the other virtues. For they are all mysteriously summed up in that little act of loving already mentioned.

26 WORK hard at it, therefore, and with all speed; hammer away at this high cloud of unknowing – and take your rest later! It is hard work and no mistake for the would-be contemplative; very hard work indeed, unless it is made easier by a special grace of God, or by the fact that one has got used to it over a long period.

But in what sense is it hard work? Obviously it is not in the devout and urgent love that is continually springing up in his will; an urge produced not automatically but by the hand of Almighty God, who is always ready to bring this about in each willing soul who has done, and is doing, all he can all the while he can in order to equip himself for this work.

Well, where is the hard work then? Without doubt it is in the stamping out all remembrance of God's creation, and in keeping them covered by that cloud of forgetting we spoke of earlier. Here is hard work, for this is our work, aided by God's grace. The other, mentioned above – the urgent movement of love – is wholly God's work. So work away on your side: I guarantee that he will not fail on his.

Work away then, with all speed! Let me see how you are standing up to it. Can you not see him waiting for you? Shame on you! Work hard but a short while, and you will soon find the vastness and the difficulty of this work begin to ease. Though in the beginning, when your devotion is negligible, it is hard and restricting, later, when devotion has come, what previously was very hard becomes much lighter, and you can relax. You even may have little effort to make, or none. For sometimes God will do it all himself. But not always, and never for any length of time, but when he likes, and as he likes. And at that time you will be happy to let him have his own way.

At such a time he may, perhaps, send out a shaft of spiritual light, which pierces this cloud of unknowing between you, and shows you some of his secrets, of which it is not permissible or possible to speak. Then will you feel your affection flame with the fire of his love, far more than I can possibly say now. For I dare not take upon myself with my blundering, earthly tongue to speak of what belongs solely to God. If I dared, I would not. But of the work that belongs to a man who is urged and helped by grace, I will gladly tell, for that is less risky!

2 7 FIRST and foremost I will tell you who should practise contemplation, and when and how and with what provisos.

If you are to ask me who should engage in this work, my answer is, 'Everyone who has truly and deliberately forsaken the world, not for the 'active' life, but for what is known as the 'contemplative' life. All such should undertake this work by grace, whoever they are, whether they have been habitual sinners or not.'

2 8 BUT if you were to ask me when they should do it, I would answer 'Not before they have cleansed their conscience of all their past sins, according to the ordinary rules of Holy Church.'

In contemplation a soul dries up the root and ground of the sin that is always there, even after one's confession, and however busy one is in holy things. Therefore, whoever would work at becoming a contemplative must first cleanse his conscience, and then, after he has made due amends, he can give himself, boldly but humbly, to contemplation. Let him recall how long he has been held back from it. For it is this work that a soul should be toiling at all his life, even if he had never sinned. All the while a soul lives in this mortal body he shall experience the obstruction of this cloud of unknowing between him and God. Moreover, as the result of original sin, he will always see and feel some of God's creatures, or their deeds, pressing in upon his mind between him and God. It is part of God's wisdom and justice that whenever man (who was sovereign and lord of his fellow creatures and yet deliberately made himself the slave of his own subjects, and turned his back on the command of God his Maker), would subsequently fulfil that command, he should see and feel those self-same creatures, which ought to be under him, proudly push in above him, between himself and God.

29 THEREFORE if a man really wants to recover the cleanness that he lost through sin, and to win through to that well-being where there is no more grief, he must patiently strive to do this work, and endure its pains, whoever he is, habitual sinner or not. Everybody finds this work extremely hard, whether he is a sinner, or quasi-innocent. But it is much more onerous for the former than for the latter, and understandably so. Yet it often happens that those who have sinned hideously and habitually come sooner to perfect contemplation than those who have not

sinned at all. This is a merciful miracle of our Lord, who has given them his special grace, to the wonderment of the whole world. I truly believe that the Day of Judgement will be a lovely day, when God will be seen clearly, and his gifts too. At that Day some of those who are now despised and thought nothing of, because they are common sinners – and perhaps even some that sin horribly – shall sit most fittingly with the saints in his sight. And some that seem to be so holy, and esteemed by men as near angels – and, perhaps, some even who never sinned mortally – shall sit most sorrowfully in the caves of hell.

You will see by this that no man should be judged by another here in this life, for the good or evil he has done. However, deeds may properly be judged whether they are good or bad, but not men.

30 By whom then shall men's deeds be judged?
Surely by those who have due authority, and the care of their souls, which has been given officially by the rule and ordaining of Holy Church, or else privately and spiritually through the special urge from the Holy Ghost in perfect love. Each one must be careful not to presume to blame and condemn other men's faults unless he feels truly moved within by the Holy Ghost. Otherwise he might very well be completely mistaken. So take care: judge yourself if you like, you and God, and your spiritual father. Leave the others well alone.

31 When you feel you have done all you can to make the proper amendment laid down by Holy Church, then get to work quick sharp! If memories of your past actions

keep coming between you and God, or any new thought or sinful impulse, you are resolutely to step over them, because of your deep love for God; you must trample them down under foot. Try to cover them with the thick cloud of forgetting, as though they had never been committed, either by you or anyone else. And, indeed, as often as they come up, push them down. And if it is really hard work you can use every 'dodge', scheme, and spiritual stratagem you can find to put them away. These arts are better learned from God by experience, than from any human teacher.

32 YET I can show you something of these spiritual arts: at least I think so. Try them out, and see if you can do better. Do everything you can to act as if you did not know that they were so strongly pushing in between you and God. Try to look, as it were, over their shoulders, seeking something else – which is God, shrouded in the cloud of unknowing. If you do so, I believe that you will soon find your hard work much easier. I believe that if this dodge is looked at in the right way, it will be found to be nothing else than a longing and desire for God, to feel and see of him what one may here below. Charity is such a desire, and it always deserves to have its way made easier.

There is another spiritual dodge to try if you wish. When you feel that you are completely powerless to put these thoughts away, cower down before them like some cringing captive overcome in battle, and reckon that it is ridiculous to fight against them any longer. In this way you surrender yourself to God while you are in the hands of your enemies, and feeling that you have been overcome for ever. Please pay special heed to this suggestion, for I think that if you try it out it will dissolve every opposition. I am quite sure that if this dodge, too, can be looked at in the right way, it will be recognized to be none other than the true knowledge and experience of the self you are; wretched, filthy, and far worse than nothing. Such knowledge and experience is humility. And this humility causes God himself to come down in his might, and avenge you of your enemies, and take you up, and fondly dry your spiritual eyes – just as a father would act towards his child, who had been about to die in the jaws of wild boar, or mad, devouring bears!

33 I SHALL not tell you any more dodges for the present, for, if you are given grace to try these out, I believe that you will soon be more able to teach me than I you! For though now I am teaching you, in all truth I know that I still have a very long way to go myself. So please help me as well as yourself.

Keep on then, and work at it as hard and as fast as you can, I beg you. Endure with all humility any suffering you have to endure, till you acquire these arts. In truth, it is your purgatory: when the pain has passed, and the skills have been given by God, and, by his grace, have become habitual, then without doubt you will have been cleansed not only from sin, but also from the suffering it causes. I am referring, of course, to the sins you have deliberately committed in the past, and not to your original sin. For the painful consequences of that will be with you till your dying day, however hard you work. But these are but a minor irritation compared with that of your deliberate sins. You will still have a lot to put up with, however. Every day original sin will produce new, fresh sinful impulses, and every day you must smite them down, and hasten to shear them off with the sharp two-edged sword of discretion. In ways like this we learn that there is no real security or true rest in this life!

Nevertheless, you cannot draw back on this account, nor yet be too dismayed if you do not always succeed. For if you are going to be given grace to destroy the painful effects of your past sins in the way I have just described – or better still in your own way if you can do it better – you can be sure that the painful consequences of your original sin, or the sinful promptings it will yet produce, will irritate you but little.

34 IF you ask me how you are to begin, I must pray Almighty God, of his grace and courtesy, to tell you himself. Indeed, it is good for you to realize that I cannot teach you. It is not to be wondered at. For this is the work of God alone, deliberately wrought in whatever soul he chooses, irrespective of the merits of that particular soul.

For without God's help neither saint nor angel can even think of wanting it. And I fancy that our Lord is willing to do this work as readily and as frequently – indeed, perhaps even more so – in those that have been lifelong sinners, as in those who have, comparatively, never grieved him very much. And he will do this, that we may recognize him to be all-merciful and almighty, and that he does what he likes, where he likes, and when he likes.

Yet he does not give this grace nor begin this work in a soul that is unwilling to receive it – though there is no soul sinful or sinless who can have this grace unless God's grace aids him. It is neither given for one's innocence, nor withheld for one's sin. Notice carefully that I say 'withheld' and not 'withdrawn'. We must beware of error here, for the more closely we approximate to truth, the more we must be on guard against error. I think my meaning is clear, but if you cannot understand it now, lay it aside till God teaches you. It will not matter.

Beware of pride: it blasphemes God and his gifts, and encourages sinners. If you were truly humble you would feel the same about the contemplative life as I do, that God gives it freely, irrespective of merits. God's gift of contemplation is such that when it is present the soul can both practise it and know it is doing so. It is impossible to come by otherwise. Capacity for contemplation is one with contemplation itself, so that only he who feels he can contemplate is able to do so. No one else can. Without this prior working of God, a soul is as it were dead, unable to covet or desire it. Since you will it, and desire it, obviously you already have it, yet it is not your will or desire that moves you, but something you are completely ignorant of, stirring you to will and desire you know not what. Please do not worry if you never know more than this, but go on ever more and more, so that you will keep advancing.

In a word, let this thing deal with you, and lead you as it will. Let it be active, and you passive. Watch it if you like, but let it alone. Do not interfere with it, as though you would help, for fear that you should spoil it all. Be the tree: let it be the carpenter. Be the house, and let it be the householder who lives there. Be willing to be blind, and give up all longing to know the why and how, for knowing will be more of a hindrance than a help. It is enough that you should feel moved lovingly by you know not what, and that in this inward urge you have no real thought for anything less than God, and that your desire is steadily and simply turned towards him.

Now if it is like this with you, you can be confident that it is God himself who is moving your will and desire, and that directly. You need have no fear, for now the devil cannot come near you. He may only stir a man's will occasionally, and then only from afar, however subtle a devil he may be. Without sufficient cause, not even a good angel can directly influence your will. In short, it is only God who can. You can understand even by what I have written here (but much more clearly by experience!) that men come to contemplation directly, without intervening 'helps'. All good helps depend upon it, but it depends on no such assistance – nor can they lead one to it.

35 NEVERTHELESS, there are helps which the apprentice in contemplation should employ, namely, Lesson, Meditation, and Orison, or, as they are more generally called, Reading, Thinking, and Praying. These three are dealt with elsewhere by another writer much better than I could deal with them, and I need not, therefore, tell you here about them. Except to say this: these three are so interwoven, that for beginners and proficients – but not for the perfect (we mean on the human level) – thinking may not be had unless reading or hearing come first. It is the same for all: clergy read books, and the man in the street 'reads' the clergy when he hears them preach the word of God. Beginners and proficients cannot pray unless they think first.

Prove it: God's word, written or spoken, can be likened to a mirror. Spiritually, the 'eye' of your soul is your reason: your conscience is your spiritual 'face'. Just as you cannot see or know that there is a dirty mark on your actual face without the aid of a mirror, or somebody telling you, so spiritually, it is impossible for a soul blinded by his frequent sins to see the dirty mark in his conscience, without reading or hearing God's word.

It follows that if a man sees where the dirty mark is on his face, either in a mirror or because someone has told him – true spiritually as well as literally – then, and not till then, he runs off to the well to wash himself. If the dirty mark is deliberate sin, the 'well' is Holy Church, and the 'water' confession, and all that goes with it. If it is a sin deeply rooted, and productive of evil impulses, then the 'well' is all-merciful God, and the 'water' prayer, and all that that involves. Thus we see that beginners and proficients cannot think unless they read or hear first, and they cannot pray without prior thinking.

36 BUT this is not the case with those who practise contemplation, that is, the readers of this book. Meditation for them is, as it were, the sudden recognition and groping awareness of their own wretchedness, or God's goodness. There has been no prior help from reading or sermons, no special meditation on anything whatever. This sudden perception and awareness is better learned from God than man. I do not mind at all if you, at this stage, have no other meditations upon your own wretchedness, or upon God's goodness (obviously I am assuming that you are moved by the grace of God in this matter, and are under direction), than such as come through the single word SIN or GOD, or some suchlike word of your own choosing. Do not analyse or expound these words with imaginative cleverness, as if, by considering their constituent parts, you would increase your devotion. I do not believe you should ever attempt this in the time of contemplation. But take the words as they are, whole. Mean by 'sin' the whole lump of it, not particularizing about any part, for it is nothing other than yourself. I think that this almost instinctive

awareness of sin, which you have solidified into a lump, and which is nothing but yourself, should make you the maddest person on earth, needing restraint! But no one looking at you would guess it from your appearance: sober in habit, giving nothing away by your expression, and doing whatever it is, sitting, walking, lying down, relaxing, standing, kneeling, in perfect calm!

37 JUST as the meditations of those who seek to live the contemplative life come without warning, so, too, do their prayers. I am thinking of their private prayers, of course, not those laid down by Holy Church. For true contemplatives could not value such prayers more, and so they use them, in the form and according to the rules laid down by the holy Fathers before us. But their own personal prayers rise spontaneously to God, without bidding of premeditation, beforehand or during their prayer.

If they are in words, as they seldom are, then they are very few words; the fewer the better. If it is a little word of one syllable, I think it is better than if it is of two, and more in accordance with the work of the Spirit. For a contemplative should always live at the highest, topmost peak spiritually.

We can illustrate this by looking at nature. A man or woman, suddenly frightened by fire, or death, or what you will, is suddenly in his extremity of spirit driven hastily and by necessity to cry or pray for help. And how does he do it? Not, surely, with a spate of words; not even in a single word of two syllables! Why? He thinks it wastes too much time to declare his urgent need and his agitation. So he bursts out in his terror with one little word, and that of a single syllable: 'Fire!' it may be, or 'Help!'

Just as this little word stirs and pierces the ears of the hearers more quickly, so too does a little word of one syllable, when it is not merely spoken or thought, but expresses also the intention in the depth of our spirit. Which is the same as the 'height' of our spirit, for in these matters height, depth, length, and breadth all mean the same. And it pierces the ears of Almighty God more quickly than any long psalm churned out unthinkingly. That is why it is written 'Short prayer penetrates heaven.'

38 WHY does it penetrate heaven, this short little prayer of one syllable? Surely because it is prayed with a full heart, in the height and depth and length and breadth of the spirit of him that prays it. In the height, for it is with all the might of his spirit; in the depth, for in this little syllable is contained all that the spirit knows; in the length, for should it always feel as it does now, it would always cry to God as it now cries; in the breadth, for it would extend to all men what it wills for itself.

At this time the soul understands what St Paul and all saints speak of – not fully, perhaps, but as much as one can at this stage of contemplation – and that is, what is the length and breadth and height and depth of the everlasting, all-loving, all-mighty, all-knowing God. God's everlastingness is his length; his love is his breadth; his might is his height; and his wisdom is his depth. No wonder that a soul moulded by grace into the close image and likeness of God his maker is so soon heard by God! Yes, even if it is a very sinful soul, who is as it were an enemy of God. If he through grace were to cry such a short syllable in the height, depth, length, and breadth of his spirit, he would always be heard because of this anguished cry, and be helped by God.

An example will show this. If you were to hear your deadly enemy in terror cry out from the depth of his being this little word 'Fire!' or 'Help!', you, without reckoning he was your enemy, out of sheer pity aroused by his despairing cry, would rise up, even on a mid-winter night, and help him put out his fire, or quieten and ease his distress. Oh Lord! since grace can make a man so merciful as to show great mercy and pity to his enemy despite his enmity, what pity and mercy shall God have for the spiritual cry of a soul that comes from its height and depth and length and breadth! God has in his nature all that man acquires by grace. And much more, incomparably more mercy will God have, since the natural endowment of a thing makes it basically more kin to eternal things than that which is given it later by grace.

39 WE must therefore pray in the height, depth, length, and breadth of our spirits. Not in many words, but in a little word of one syllable. What shall this word be? Surely such a word as is suited to the nature of prayer itself. And what word is that? First let us see what prayer is in itself, and then we shall know more clearly what word will best suit its nature.

In itself prayer is nothing else than a devout setting of our will in the direction of God in order to get good, and remove evil. Since all evil is summed up in sin, considered causally or essentially, when we pray with intention for the removing of evil, we should neither say, think, nor mean any more than this little word 'sin'. And if we pray with intention for the acquiring of goodness, let us pray, in word or thought or desire, no other word than 'God'. For in God is all good, for he is its beginning and its being. Do not be

surprised then that I set these words before all others. If I
could find any shorter words which would sum up fully
the thought of good or evil as these words do, or if I had
been led by God to take some other words, then I would
have used those and left these. And that is my advice for
you too.

But don't study these words, for you will never achieve
your object so, or come to contemplation; it is never
attained by study, but only by grace. Take no other words
for your prayer, despite all I have said, than those that God
leads you to use. Yet if God does lead you to these, my
advice is not to let them go, that is, if you are using words
at all in your prayer: not otherwise. They are very short
words. But though shortness of prayer is greatly to be
recommended here, it does not mean that the frequency of
prayer is to be lessened. For as I have said, it is prayed in the
length of one's spirit, so that it never stops until such time
as it has fully attained what it longs for. We can turn to our
terrified man or woman for an example. They never stop
crying their little words 'Help!' or 'Fire!' till such time as
they have got all the help they need in their trouble.

40 In the same way you should fill your spirit with
the inner meaning of the single word 'sin', without analys-
ing what kind it is, venial or mortal, or pride, anger, envy,
avarice, sloth, gluttony, or lust. What does it matter to
contemplatives what sort of a sin it is, or how great? For
when they are engaged in contemplation, they think all
sins alike are great in themselves, when the smallest sin
separates them from God, and prevents spiritual peace.

Feel sin in its totality – as a lump – without specifying any
particular part, and that all of it is you. And then cry

ceaselessly in your spirit this one thing: 'Sin! Sin! Sin! Help! Help! Help!' This spiritual cry is better learned from God by experience than from any man by word. It is best when it is entirely spiritual, unpremeditated and unuttered. On occasion perhaps the over-full heart will burst out into words, because body and soul alike are filled with sorrow, and the burden of sin.

In the same way too you should use this little word 'God'. Fill your spirit with its inner meaning, without considering any one of his works in particular, for example, whether it is good, better, or best of all, or whether it is physical or spiritual, or whether it is a virtue wrought in a man's soul by grace, and in this last case without classifying it as humility or charity, patience or abstinence, hope, faith, self-control, chastity, or voluntary poverty.

What does all this matter to contemplatives? For in God they find and experience every virtue. In him is everything: he made it and he maintains it. They know that if they have God they have all good, and so they covet no good thing in particular, but only good God. Do the same, as far as you can by grace, and mean God wholeheartedly, and the whole of him. So that nothing works in your mind or will, but God alone.

And because all the while you live this wretched life you have to experience in some sort this filthy and nauseating lump of sin, part and parcel of yourself, you must constantly revert to these two words in turn, 'sin' and 'God'. With the knowledge that if you had God you would not have sin, and if you had not sin, then you would have God!

41 IF you are to ask me what discretion you should exercise in this work, my answer is 'None whatever!' In

everything else you do, you have to use your own discretion, as, for example, in the matter of food and drink and sleep and keeping warm or cool, the time you spend in praying or reading, your conversations with your fellow Christians. In all these you have to use discretion, so that they are not too much or too little. But in this work, cast discretion to the wind! I want you never to give this work up all the while you live.

I am not saying that you will always come to it fresh, for that cannot be. Sometimes illness or some other upset of body or soul, or natural necessity will prove a real hindrance, and often prevent you from contemplating. But you should always be at this work, both 'on duty' and 'off', in intention if not in reality. For the love of God beware of illness as much as you can, so that as far as possible your self is not the cause of any weakness. I tell you the truth when I say that this work demands great serenity, an integrated and pure disposition, in soul and in body.

So for the love of God control your body and soul alike with great care, and keep as fit as you can. Should illness come in spite of everything, have patience and wait humbly for God's mercy. That is all that is asked. For I tell the truth when I say that patience in sickness and other kinds of tribulation often pleases God far more than any pleasant devotion you might show in health.

42 You will ask me, perhaps, how you are to control yourself with due care in the matter of food and drink and sleep and so on. My answer is brief: 'Take what comes!' Do this thing without ceasing and without care day by day, and you will know well enough, with a real discretion, when to begin and when to stop in everything else. I

cannot believe that a soul who goes on in this work with complete abandon, day and night, will make mistakes in mundane matters. If he does, he is, I think, the type who always will get things wrong.

Therefore, if I am able to give a vital and wholehearted attention to this spiritual activity within my soul, I can then view my eating and drinking, my sleep and conversation and so on with comparative indifference. I would rather acquire a right discretion in these matters by such indifference, than by giving them my close attention, and weighing carefully all their pros and cons. Indeed, I could never bring it about in such a way, for all I might do or say. Let men say what they will: experience teaches. Therefore lift your heart up with this blind upsurge of love, and consider now 'sin', and now 'God'. God you want to have; sin you want to lose. You lack God: you know all about sin. Good God help you now, for it is now that you have need of him.

43 SEE to it that there is nothing at work in your mind or will but only God. Try to suppress all knowledge and feeling of anything less than God, and trample it down deep under the cloud of forgetting. You must understand that in this business you are to forget not only all other things than yourself (and their doings – and your own!) but to forget also yourself, and even the things you have done for the sake of God. For it is the way of the perfect lover not only to love what he loves more than himself, but also in some sort to hate himself for the sake of what he loves.

So you are to do with yourself. You must loathe and tire of all that goes on in your mind and your will unless it is God. For otherwise surely whatever it is is between you and God. No wonder you loathe and hate thinking about yourself when you always feel your sin to be a filthy and nauseating lump – you do not particularize – between you and God, and that that lump is yourself. For you are to think of it as being identified with yourself: inseparable from you.

So crush all knowledge and experience of all forms of created things, and of yourself above all. For it is on your own self knowledge and experience that the knowledge and experience of everything else depend. Alongside this self-regard everything else is quickly forgotten. For if you will take the trouble to test it, you will find that when all other things and activities have been forgotten (even your own) there still remains between you and God the stark awareness of your own existence. And this awareness, too, must go, before you experience contemplation in its perfection.

44 You will ask me next how to destroy this stark awareness of your own existence. For you are thinking that if it were destroyed all other difficulties would vanish too. And you would be right. All the same my answer must be that without God's very special and freely given grace, and your own complete and willing readiness to receive it, this stark awareness of yourself cannot possibly be destroyed. And this readiness is nothing else than a strong, deep sorrow of spirit.

But in this sorrow you need to exercise discretion: you must beware of imposing undue strain on your body or soul at this time. Rather, sit quite still, mute as if asleep, absorbed and sunk in sorrow. This is true sorrow, perfect sorrow, and all will go well if you can achieve sorrow to this degree. Everyone has something to sorrow over, but none more than he who knows and feels that he is.[1] All other sorrow in comparison with this is a travesty of the real thing. For he experiences true sorrow, who knows and feels not only what he is, but that he is. Let him who has never felt this sorrow be sorry indeed, for he does not yet know what perfect sorrow is. Such sorrow, when we have it, cleanses the soul not only of sin, but also of the suffering its sin has deserved. And it makes the soul ready to receive that joy which is such that it takes from a man all awareness of his own existence.

When this sorrow is genuine it is full of holy longing. Without such longing no one on earth could cope with it, or endure it. For were the soul not strengthened by its good endeavours, it would be unable to stand the pain that the awareness of its own existence brings. For as often as in his purity of heart a man would know the true awareness of God (as much as may be possible here below) and then feels he may not (because he finds his awareness held and filled with the filthy and nauseating lump of himself – which has got to be hated, despised, and forsaken if he would be God's perfect disciple, as the Lord himself taught on the Mount of Perfection) just as often he goes nearly mad with sorrow. So much so that he weeps and wails, oppresses, curses, and denounces himself. In a word, he thinks the burden he carries is so heavy that he does not mind what happens to him so long as God is pleased. Yet in all this sorrow he does not want to cease existing: that would be devil's madness, and contempt of God. Though he continues longing to be free of its awareness, he wants very much to go on in existence, and he gives God heartfelt thanks for this precious gift.

This sorrow and longing every soul must know and

1. i.e. that he exists over and against God.

experience in some form or other. God condescends to teach his spiritual disciples according to his good will. There must be a corresponding readiness in body and soul, in development and disposition, before they can be perfectly united with him in perfect love, as far as is possible in this life, and if God permits.

45 BUT a word of warning. It is quite possible for a young disciple, inexperienced and untested spiritually, to be deceived. Unless he is alive to the situation, and has grace to stop what he is doing and take advice humbly, he may be destroyed physically and get fantastic ideas spiritually. And withal be proud, and materialistic, and inquisitive.

It may be like this that he is deceived: A young man or woman just starting in the school of devotion hears someone read or speak about this sorrow and longing: how a man shall lift up his heart to God, and continually long to feel his love. And immediately in their silly minds they understand these words not in the intended spiritual sense, but in a physical and material, and they strain their natural hearts outrageously in their breasts! And because they are without grace, and are proud and spiritually inquisitive they strain their whole nervous system in untutored, animal ways, and thus they quickly get tired with a sort of physical and spiritual torpor. This causes them to turn from the life which is within and seek empty, false, and physical comforts from outside, ostensibly for the recreation of body and soul. Or, if they do not do this, they get (and deserve to get, because of their spiritual obtuseness and the physical irritation caused by the pretended work of the spirit – in fact, of course, it is animal) an unnatural glow within themselves, caused by the abuse of their bodies, or their sham spirituality. Or, again, they experience a spurious warmth, engendered by the fiend, their spiritual enemy through their pride, and materialism, and spiritual dabbling.

And yet, maybe, they imagine it to be the fire of love, lighted and fanned by the grace and goodness of the Holy Ghost. In truth, from this falsehood many evils spring: much hypocrisy and heresy and error. For hot on the heels of false experience comes false knowledge in the school of the fiend, just as true experience is followed by true knowledge in the school of God. For I tell you truly that the devil has his contemplatives as God has his.

These beguiling, false experiences and this false knowledge have as many different and surprising varieties as there are temperaments and states to be deceived. So too have the true experiences and knowledge of the saved. But I will put here no more spiritual lies than those I think you will be attacked with if you ever mean to become a contemplative. For what does it help you to know how clergy and men and women of differing backgrounds from your own are led astray? Surely not at all. So I am telling you no more than those that will happen to you if you undertake this work. And I tell you so that you can be on your guard if they should attack you on your way.

46 So for the love of God be careful in this matter, and do not overstrain yourself emotionally or beyond your strength. Work with eager enjoyment rather than with brute force. The more eager your work, the more humble and spiritual it becomes; the more crude, the more material and animal. So beware. For surely the animal (in our case

the animal heart) that dares to touch the high mountain of contemplation shall be driven off with stones.[1] Stones are hard dry things, and where they hit, they hurt. Surely such violent strainings are inseparable from a materialistic and physical outlook, and are dry for lack of the dew of grace. They sorely hurt the silly soul, and it festers in feigned and fiendish fantasies! So beware of behaving wildly like some animal, and learn to love God with quiet, eager joy, at rest in body as in soul. Remember your manners, and wait humbly upon our Lord's will. Do not snatch at it, like some famished dog, however much you hunger for it. If I may use a funny example, I would suggest you do all you can to cloak your great and ungoverned spiritual urge; as though you were altogether unwilling that he should know how very glad you would be to see him, to have him, to feel him.

Perhaps you think I am speaking childishly or playfully. Yet I believe that whoever had the grace to put what I say into practice would have a lovely game spiritually with him – just as an earthly father does with his child, hugging and kissing him – and would be glad to have it so.

47 DO not be surprised that I speak about this in a childlike fashion, and, as it were, foolishly, with no sense of fitness. I do it for certain reasons, and because I think I have been moved for some time to feel, think, and speak about it in this sort of way, both to some of my other special friends in God, and now to you.

One reason why I bid you hide from God the desire of your heart is this: I think it is a clearer way of bringing to his notice what you are aiming at, and it is more beneficial

1. Heb. 12:20, Ex. 19:13.

for you, and will sooner fulfil your desire, than any other sort of demonstration.

Another reason is this: by such a 'hidden demonstration' I want to get you away from the violence of emotional reaction, into the purity and depth of spiritual experience. And so ultimately to help you to tie that spiritual knot of burning love between you and God, in spiritual oneness and harmony of will.

You know well that God is a spirit, and that whoever would be made one with him must be in truth and in depth of spirit far removed from any misleading bodily thing. It is true that everything is known to God, and that nothing can be hidden from his knowledge, physical or spiritual. But since he is a spirit, that thing which is hidden in the depths of a man's spirit is to him even more clearly known and obvious than is a thing that is intermixed with the bodily. For by its nature every physical thing is farther from God than any spiritual. For this reason it would seem that all the while our longing has any sort of natural element in it (as is the case when we strain and stress ourselves emotionally and spiritually at one and the same moment) it is that much farther from God than it would be if there had been greater devotion, and more sober eagerness, purity, and spiritual depth.

Here you may see something, at any rate partially, of the reason why I tell you to cloak and hide from God, like a child playing a game, the urgency of your longing. At the same time, however, I tell you not to hide it completely. That would be the advice of a fool to tell you to do what in any case cannot be done! Yet I still tell you to do what you can to hide it! Why do I say this? Because I want you to plunge it deep down into your spirit, far removed from any material admixture which would make it less spiritual, and that much farther from God. And, too, because I know well that the more spiritual your soul becomes, the less emotional are its desires, and the nearer to God, and more pleasing to him, and more clearly noticeable. Not that at one time he sees anything more clearly than at another – for he is unchanging – but because the soul is more like him when it is pure in spirit, for he is a spirit.

There is another reason why I tell you to do what you can not to let him know. You and I, and all like us, are so apt to conceive what is said spiritually in material terms, that had I, perchance, told you to show God the urgency that is in your heart, you would have expressed it physically, by your expression, or voice, or word, or in some other instinctive action of the body in the same way that you show what is in your inmost heart to a friend – and to that extent your action would have been a mixed one. For we show a thing to man in one way, and to God in another.

48 I AM not saying this because I want you to stop praying vocally whenever you are so moved, or to prevent you breaking out, in your overflowing devotion of soul, in normal speech to God with some appropriate word of good, such as 'Good Jesus!' 'Lovely Jesus!' 'Sweet Jesus!' and so on. No, God forbid you understand me to mean this! Really I do not mean this. God forbid that I should part what he has joined, the body and spirit. For God wants to be served with body and soul, both together, as is right, and to give man his heavenly reward in body as well as in soul. And as a foretaste of that reward, he will on occasion inflame the actual body of his devout servant – and not once or twice, but perhaps often, and when he likes –

with very wonderful sweetness and consolation. Not all of this comes from outside into our bodies through the windows of our intellect, but rather from within, rising and springing from the abundance of spiritual gladness, and true devotion of soul. Such comfort and such sweetness should not be held suspect, and, to say no more, I believe that he who enjoys it cannot regard it so. But all other comforts, sounds, gladness, sweetness that come suddenly to you from outside, whose origin you do not know, please do suspect! They can be good or evil; the work of a good angel if good, and of an evil angel if evil. They will not be evil if those misleading intellectual questionings and unregulated emotional strainings have been put away; in such ways as I have suggested, or in better ways if you know them. And why is that? Surely it is that the cause of this comfort is the devout movement of love, dwelling in a pure spirit. It is wrought by the hand of Almighty God, directly in the soul. Therefore it must always be independent of one's imagination, or of the wrong ideas a man may acquire in this life.

Of the other comforts, sounds and sweetnesses, and how to distinguish good from evil I do not intend to tell you for the moment. Not because I think it unnecessary, but because you can find it set out elsewhere by somebody else a thousand times better than I could say or write. You can find all that I set out here dealt with far better there. But what of it? I shall not cease from, nor weary of, seeking to meet your wants, and that longing urge of your spirit, which you have shown me you possess earlier in your words, and now in your actions.

But this I may say about those sounds and sweetnesses that come to us through the windows of our intellect, and which may be good or evil. Practise continually this blind, devout, eager outgoing of love that I speak about, and then

I have no doubt it will be quite capable of telling you about them itself. And if you are astonished, partly if not wholly, when they first come – and that is because you are not used to them – it will at least do this for you: it will give your heart such solidity that you will never give full credence to them, until you are absolutely sure of them, either through the inner, wonderful approval of the Spirit of God, or from the outside advice of some discreet director.

49 So I beg you to incline with all eagerness to this lowly movement of love which is in your heart, and to follow it; it will be your guide in this life, and bring you to the bliss of heaven in the next. It is the essence of all good living, and without it no good work may be begun or ended. It is nothing other than a good will in harmony with God, and a kind of pleasure and gladness which you experience in your will at all that he does.

Such a goodwill is the substance of all perfection. All sweetness and comfort, both physical and spiritual, however holy they may be, in comparison with this are accidents and unessential which depend upon this good will. I call them 'accidents' because they may be present or not without touching the good will. I am thinking of this life, of course, because in heaven they will be inseparably united with their substance, as will be the body in which they work with the soul. Their substance here below is the good, spiritual will. I am quite sure that the man who, as far as is possible in this life, has this perfect will is as happy and glad not to have consolations and sweetness as to have them, if God's will is so.

50 IN this way you can see that we must concentrate our whole attention on this lowly movement of love in our will. To all other forms of sweetness or consolation, however pleasant or holy (if we may be allowed to put it in this way) we should show a sort of indifference. If they come, welcome them; but do not depend on them, because they are weakening things; it takes too much out of you to stay for long in such sweet feelings and tears. And you may even be tempted to love God for the sake of having them. You will know if this is so by seeing whether you complain unduly when they are absent. And if you do, your love is not yet pure or perfect. For a love that is pure and perfect, though it admits that the body is sustained and consoled when such sweet feelings or tears are present, does not complain when they are missing, but is really pleased not to have them, if it is the will of God. And yet in some people contemplation is normally accompanied by consolations of this sort, while there are others who have such sweetness and comfort but seldom.

This all depends upon the purpose and ordering of God, and is according to the need or good of each different person. There are people who are so weak and sensitive spiritually that, unless they were comforted by some such sweetness, they would find it impossible to endure the various temptations and tribulations that they have to suffer and struggle with in life, and which come from their physical and spiritual foes. And there are some who are so weak constitutionally that they cannot perform an adequate penance for their cleansing. Our Lord in his grace cleanses such folk in their spirit with sweet emotions and tears. Yet on the other hand there are those who are so strong spiritually that they can glean sufficient comfort from their own souls – in offering up this reverent, humble, outreaching love, and their obedient will – and have little need to be sustained with sweet emotions. Which of these is holier or dearer to God, he knows, and I do not.

51 THEREFORE attend in humility to this unseeing movement of love in your heart. I don't mean your physical heart, of course, but your spiritual one, that is, your will. Be careful not to interpret physically what is meant spiritually. The earthly and physical fancies of inventive imaginations are very fruitful of error.

You can see an example of this in the things I have been speaking of, your hiding from God your desire for him as far as you are able. If, for example, I had told you to show your desire to him, you would have understood it much more literally than you do when I tell you to hide it. For now you are fully aware that the thing that is deliberately hidden is a thing deep down in the spirit. So I think it is very important to be extremely careful in the way we understand what has been intended spiritually, that we interpret it so, and not literally. And we have got to take particular care with those two words, 'in' and 'up'. The misunderstanding of these words has caused much error and wrong in would-be contemplatives, I fancy. I know something of this by experience, and something by hearsay, and of these errors I now intend to say a little.

A young disciple in God's school, newly converted, thinks that, because of the short time he has given to penance and prayer – the result of the advice of his confessor – he can therefore engage in contemplation, about which he has heard people speak or read, or perhaps has read himself. When people like this hear of 'contemplation', and particularly of this sort of pronouncement, that 'a man shall gather all his powers within himself', or how 'he shall climb above himself', immediately because of their spiritual blindness and literal and perverse outlook, they misunderstand these words, and think that because they find within themselves an innate desire for mystical things they are therefore called to such a work by grace. So that if their director will not agree that they shall begin contemplating they promptly find fault with him, and think – and possibly say to others who are likeminded – they can find no one who really understands them. So at once and too soon, with the daring and presumption that go with a perverse intellect, they give up humble prayer and penance, and begin what they think is the real spiritual work for their soul – and this, if they do it truly, is neither physical nor spiritual. Briefly, it is an unnatural thing, and the devil is its chief agent. It is the quickest way to die, physically and spiritually, for it is madness, not wisdom, and drives a man mad. And yet they do not think so, for they mean in this work to think of nothing but God.

52 THE madness I speak of is effected like this: they read and hear it said that they should stop the 'exterior' working with their mind, and work interiorly. And because they do not know what this 'interior' work means, they do it wrong. For they turn their actual physical minds inwards to their bodies, which is an unnatural thing, and they strain as if to see spiritually with their physical eyes, and to hear within with their outward ears, and to smell and taste and feel and so on inwardly in the same way. So they pervert the natural order, and with this false ingenuity they put their minds to such unnecessary strains that ultimately their brains are turned. And at once the devil is able to

deceive them with false lights and sounds, sweet odours and wonderful tastes, glowing and burning in their hearts or stomachs, backs or loins or limbs.

In all this make-believe they imagine they are peacefully contemplating their God, unhindered by vain thoughts. So they are, in a fashion, for they are so stuffed with falsehood that a little extra vanity cannot disturb them. Why? Because it is the same devil that is working on them now as would be tempting them if they were on the right road. You know very well that he will not get in his own way. He does not remove all thought of God from them, lest they should become suspicious.

53 THE expressions and gestures which this counterfeit contemplation (or anything similar) produces in those that are led astray are wonderful to behold, much more so than those of God's true disciples, for these latter are always most proper in their behaviour, physical or spiritual. But not so with these others! Whoever cares to look at them as they sit at such a time, will see them staring (if their eyes are open) as though they were mad, and sniggering as if they saw the devil. (It is good for them to beware, for the fiend truly is not far away!) Some squint as though they were silly sheep that have been banged on the head, and were going soon to die. Some hang their heads on one side as if they had got a worm in their ear. Some squeak when they should speak, as if they had no spirit – the proper condition for a hypocrite! Some cry and whine, because they are in such an anxious hurry to say what they think – heretics are like this, and all who with presumptuous and ingenious minds maintain error.

If a man saw everything they did he would see much

disorderly and unseemly behaviour. Yet there are some clever enough to restrain themselves in general before the people. But if they could be seen at home, I reckon there would be no hiding them. And I also reckon that whoever directly contradicted their opinion would soon see them burst out somewhere or other ... and yet they think that all they do is done for the love of God, and to maintain truth! I really believe that unless God works a miracle of mercy to make them stop, they will 'love God' like this for so long that they will end by going to the devil, raving mad. I am not saying that the devil has a servant so perfect that he is deceived and infected with all the delusion I describe here, yet it is possible for one, perhaps many, to be infected with them all. I do say, however, that though he may not possess any complete hypocrite or heretic here on earth, he is responsible for some that I have mentioned, or shall mention, God permitting.

For some men are so prone to these curious tricks of deportment that, when they are listening to anything, they twist their heads quaintly on one side, and stick their chins up. Mouth agape, they give the impression that they would hear with their mouths, and not with their ears! Some when they speak add emphasis by pointing with their fingers, either on the fingers of the other hand, or on their breast, or on that of the person they are speaking to. Some can neither sit still, stand still, nor lie still, without waggling their feet or fidgeting with their hands. Some speak with great rowing movements of their arms, as though they had to swim an ocean. Some are everlastingly giggling and laughing at every other word they speak, as though they were fast women, or common clowns who didn't know how to behave. Far better to have a modest expression, and to comport oneself with sobriety and quietness, and with a genuine happiness.

I am not saying that all these unseemly gestures are great sins in themselves, nor that those who perform them are great sinners. But I do say that if these antics gain the upper hand, so that a man cannot dispense with them they are then a sure sign of pride, perverted knowledge, unregulated showing off, and sinful curiosity. And more particularly do they reveal an unstable heart, and a restless mind, and an inability to do what this book is urging. This is the only reason why I set out these errors here, so that a contemplative can test his progress by them.

54 ALL who engage in this work of contemplation find that it has a good effect on the body as well as on the soul, for it makes them attractive in the eyes of all who see them. So much so that the ugliest person alive who becomes, by grace, a contemplative finds that he suddenly (and again by grace) is different, and that every good man he sees is glad and happy to have his friendship, and is spiritually refreshed, and helped nearer God by his company.

Therefore seek to get this gift by grace; for whoever really has it will be well able to control both himself and his possessions by virtue of it. It gives him discernment, when he needs it, to read people's needs and characters. It gives him the knack of being at home with everyone he talks to, habitual sinner or not, without sinning himself . . . to the astonishment of the onlooker, and with a magnetic effect on others, drawing them by grace to the same spiritual work that he practises.

His face and his words are full of spiritual wisdom, fervent and fruitful, assured and free from falsehood, far from feigned and affected hypocrites. For there are those who concentrate all their energies on learning how to speak weightily and to avoid making fools of themselves, with many humble bleats and displays of devotion. They are more anxious to seem holy in the sight of men than in the sight of God and his angels. Why, these people will worry and grieve more over unorthodox ritual, or the speaking of an unseemly or unsuitable word, than they will for a thousand vain thoughts or nauseating and sinful impulses, which they have deliberately gathered to themselves, or recklessly indulged in in the sight of God, and the saints and angels in heaven. Ah, Lord God! where there are so many humble bleats without, there must be pride within. I am ready to grant that it is appropriate and seemly for those who are genuinely humble to express the humility of their heart outwardly in words and behaviour. But I cannot say they should be expressed in quavering or high-pitched voices, contrary to the natural disposition of the speaker. For if they are genuine, they are spoken with sincerity, and the speaker's voice is as sound as his spirit. If a man who has naturally a loud and powerful voice, speaks in a pathetic and high pitched voice (assuming he is not ill, or is not talking with God or his confessor!) then it is a plain token of hypocrisy in young or old alike.

What more shall I say of these poisonous errors? Unless they have grace to leave off this hypocritical bleating, I really believe that between the secret pride of their inmost hearts, and the humble words on their lips, their pitiable souls will very soon sink with sorrow.

55 THE fiend will deceive some men in this way; in a most remarkable fashion he will set them on fire to maintain the law of God and to destroy sin in all other men. He

will never tempt them with anything that is openly evil. He makes them like those busy ecclesiastics who watch over every condition of our Christian life, as an abbot does over his monks. For they do not hesitate to reprove us all for our faults, just as if they had the cure of souls. For the sake of God they think they dare not do otherwise than declare the faults they see. They say they have been moved to do so by fervent charity, and by the love of God that is in their hearts. But they lie. It is the fire of hell which is welling up in their minds and imaginations.

That this is true seems to be shown by what follows: the devil is a spirit, and no more has a body than has an angel. Yet when he or an angel assumes, by God's leave, a body in order to do something for a human being, he still retains a 'recognizable something' of his essential self. Scripture provides examples. Whenever an angel was sent in bodily form in the Old or the New Testament, it was always shown, either by his name or by something he did or revealed, what his essential nature or errand was. It is the same with the fiend. When he appears in bodily shape, he betrays in some visible way what his servants are in spirit.

Let me take only one example of this. I understand from followers of spiritualism – necromancers who claim to know how to call up wicked spirits, and to whom the fiend has appeared in physical form, that in whatever likeness he appears, he has never more than one nostril, which is great and wide, and that he will gladly turn it up so that a man can see through to his brain. And his brain is nothing else than the fire of hell, for the fiend cannot have any other brain. And if he can make a man look, he wants no better. For when he looks he goes mad for ever. But your experienced practitioner of necromancy knows this well enough, and can so order things that he suffers no harm.

So it is as I say, and have said, that whenever the devil

assumes human shape he betrays in some visible way what his servants are in spirit. For he so inflames the imagination of his contemplatives with the fire of hell that suddenly, in the most tactless fashion, they will launch their peculiar views, and without any sort of waiting will take upon themselves to blame other men's faults before they know enough to do so. That division in a man's nose, which separates one nostril from the other, suggests that a man should have spiritual insight, and know how to distinguish the good from the evil, the evil from the worse, the good from the better, before he passes judgement of anything that he has heard or seen done around him. (A man's brain spiritually signifies the imagination, for through its nature it dwells and works in the head.)

56 THERE are some who, though they do not fall into the error I have just mentioned, yet because of their pride, their natural ingenuity of mind, and their erudition, give up the doctrine and counsel of Holy Church as generally held. These men and their supporters lean too much on their own learning. And because they were never grounded in this humble, 'blind', experience, and in virtuous living, they deserve to have a false experience, counterfeited and produced by their spiritual enemy. So that at last they burst out and blaspheme all the saints, sacraments, statutes, and ordinances of Holy Church. Gross worldlings, who think that the statutes of Holy Church are too hard to help them amend their lives, go over to these heretics too soon and too readily, and vigorously support them; all because they think that they lead them by a more comfortable way than that laid down by Holy Church.

Now I really believe that those who will not go the hard

way to heaven will go the comfortable way to hell . . . as we shall all find out for ourselves. I believe that if we could see for ourselves the condition of these heretics and their supporters as they will be at the Last Day, we should see them bowed down not only with the burden of their bare-faced effrontery in upholding error but also with great and horrible sins of the world and of the flesh that have been done in secret. For it is said of them that for all their apparent virtue, in private they will be found to be both filthy and debauched, and rightly called the disciples of Antichrist.

57 BUT no more of this for the time being; we must move on, and see how these presumptuous young disciples misinterpret this other word, 'up'. For if they read, or hear it read or spoken about, that men should lift up their hearts unto God, at once they are star-gazing as if they wanted to get past the moon, and listening to hear an angel sing out of heaven. In their mental fantasies they penetrate to the planets, and make a hole in the firmament, and look through! They make a God to their liking, and give him rich clothes, and set him on a throne, and it is all much odder than any painting! And they make angels have human shapes, and plant them about, each one with a different musical instrument. Much odder than has ever been heard or seen here below!

Some of these men the devil will deceive quite wonder-fully. For he sends a sort of dew – they think it is angels' food – coming out of the air as it were, and falling gently and sweetly into their mouths! They get the habit therefore of sitting gaping, as though they were catching flies! Now all this is really only pious fraud, for their souls at such times are empty of real devotion. In their hearts is much vanity and error, caused by their fantastic practices. So much so that often the devil will deceive their ears with quaint sounds, their eyes with quaint lights and shinings, their noses with wonderful smells – and they are all false!

And yet they don't see it. They find examples for this looking-upward business in, for example, St Martin, who saw by revelation God wearing his cloak among all his angels, or in St Stephen, who saw our Lord standing in heaven, or in many others. And in Christ himself who was seen by his disciples ascending bodily to heaven. Therefore, say they, we should look up. I readily grant that in our bodily observance we should lift up our eyes and our hands if the spirit moves. But I am saying that the work of our spirit does not go up or down, sideways, forward, or backward, like some physical thing. Because our work is a spiritual work, and not physical; nor is it achieved in a physical fashion.

58 WITH regard to what they say about St Martin and St Stephen: though they saw such things with their physical eyes, it was clearly a miracle, and was demonstrating a spiritual truth. They know perfectly well that St Martin's cloak never really was worn by Christ, who needed it to keep out the cold, but was only worn miraculously, and for a reminder to all of us who can be saved, and who are united spiritually to the body of Christ. Whoever they are that out of love for God clothe a poor man, or do any sort of good to the needy, whether the good is physical or spiritual, they may be quite sure that they do it spiritually to Christ; and they will be rewarded for it as really as if they had done it actually to him. He says

this himself in the Gospel. Yet he thought it not enough, until he subsequently confirmed it by a miracle; and so he showed himself to St Martin in a special revelation. All the visions that men see here in human shape have spiritual meanings. And I fancy that if those who saw them had been sufficiently spiritual, or could have come by their meaning spiritually, they would never have been shown physically. Therefore let us strip off the husk, and eat the sweet kernel.

But how? Not as these heretics do, for they have been likened to those mad folk whose custom it is when they have drunk from some beautiful cup to throw it at the wall and break it; we are not going to do this sort of thing, if we mean to make progress. For we who feed on its fruit are not going to despise the tree, nor when we drink break the cup we have drunk from. I would call the tree and the cup a miracle that we can see, like all those outward observances which help and do not hinder the spirit. I would call the fruit and the drink the spiritual meaning behind these visible miracles, these proper outward observances, like the lifting up of our eyes and hands towards heaven. If they are done at the bidding of the spirit, they are good; otherwise it is hypocrisy, and they are false. If they are sincere and contain spiritual fruit, why despise them? For men will kiss the cup that holds wine.

And what if our Lord, ascending bodily to heaven, was seen by the physical eyes of his mother and his disciples on the way up into the clouds? Are we therefore, when we contemplate, to stare upwards, looking if we might see him sitting down in heaven, or standing, like St Stephen did? No. Surely he did not reveal himself in human guise to St Stephen in order to teach us in our spiritual life to look physically up to heaven, if perchance we might see him too, as did St Stephen, standing, sitting, or lying down. For what his body is doing in heaven – whether it is standing, sitting, or lying – no one knows. Nor do we need to know more than that his body is inseparably united with his soul. His body and soul, that is, his Manhood, in turn is inseparably united with the Godhead. We do not need to know about his sitting, standing, or lying, but that he is there doing what he likes, and that he is, in his body, whatever is best for him to be. For if he shows himself in any of these postures in a physical vision to anybody, it is done for some spiritual purpose, and not because he is actually adopting that posture in heaven.

An example will illustrate: The word 'standing' implies a readiness to help. Thus it is frequently said by one friend to another when he is engaged in physical combat, 'Bear up, old man; fight hard, and don't give up too easily. I'll stand by you.' He is not only meaning physical standing, for perhaps this is a cavalry battle, charging forward and not stationary. But he means, when he says he will stand by him, that he will be ready to help him. This is the reason why our Lord showed himself in a physical way in heaven to St Stephen in his martyrdom, and not to give us an example to look up to heaven. As if he were saying to St Stephen, the representative of all who suffer persecution for love of him, 'Stephen, as truly as I open the firmament of heaven and let you see me standing physically, so you may trust that just as truly I am standing by you spiritually, by the power of my Godhead, ready to help you. Therefore stand firm in the faith, and endure bravely the dreadful hurt of those hard stones. For I shall crown you in heaven as a reward, and not you only, but all who suffer persecution in any way for my sake.'

So you can see that these outward displays were for spiritual purposes.

59 AND if you are going to refer me to our Lord's Ascension, and say it must have physical significance as well as spiritual, seeing it was a physical body that ascended, and he is true God and true Man, my answer is that he had been dead, and then was clothed with immortality; and so shall we be at the Day of Judgement. At that time we shall be so rarefied in our body-and-soul, that we shall be able to go physically wherever we will as swiftly as we can now go anywhere mentally in thought. Up, down, sideways, backwards, forwards – it will be all the same to us, and good, so the scholars say. But at the present time you cannot go to heaven physically, but only spiritually. And it is so really spiritual that it is not physical at all: neither above or below us, beside or behind or before.

Make quite sure that all those who mean to live the spiritual life, and particularly that sort outlined in this book, when they read 'lift up' or 'go in', or that the work of this book is called 'a moving', clearly understand that this moving does not reach up or go in in a physical sense, and the movement is not from one place to another! Even if it is sometimes called 'a rest', they must not think that it means staying in one place and not leaving it. For contemplative perfection is so fine and so spiritual in itself, that if we properly understood it, we would realize it to be poles apart from any physical movement or place.

It might more reasonably be called a sudden 'changing' rather than a movement. For in contemplative praying we should forget all about time and place and body. So be careful not to take the physical ascension of Christ as an example, so that you try to lift your imagination physically upwards, as if you would climb past the moon! It cannot be so spiritually. If you were going to ascend physically into heaven like Christ, then you might use it as an example. But no one can do that except God, as he says, 'No man can ascend to heaven but he that came down from heaven, and became man for the love of men.'[1] Even if it were possible, and it isn't, it could only be for fuller spiritual activity, and solely by the power of the spirit, completely removed from all physical strain and stress on our imagination, which would make it go 'up', 'in', 'sideways' or what.

So leave such error alone: it cannot be so.

60 Now perhaps you are saying, 'But how do you arrive at these conclusions?' For you are thinking you have real evidence that heaven is up above, for Christ ascended physically upwards, and, later, sent the Holy Spirit, as he promised, from above, unseen by any disciple. And we believe this. And therefore, you think, with this real evidence before you, why should you not direct your mind literally upward when you pray?

I will answer this as best I can, however inadequately. Since it had to be that Christ should ascend physically, and then send the Holy Spirit in tangible form, it was more suitable that it should be 'upwards', and 'from above', than it should be 'downwards' and 'from beneath', 'from behind, from the front, or from the sides'. Apart from this matter of suitability, there was no more need for him to have gone upwards than downwards, the way is so near. For, spiritually, heaven is as near down as up, up as down, behind as before, before as behind, on this side as on that! So that whoever really wanted to be in heaven, he is there and then in heaven spiritually. For we run the high way (and the quickest) to heaven on our desires, and not on our

1. John 3:13.

two feet. So St Paul speaks for himself and many others when he says that although our bodies are actually here on earth, we are living in heaven.[1] He is meaning their love and their desire, which is, spiritually, their life. Surely the soul is as truly there where the object of its love is, as it is in its body which depends on it, and to which it gives life. If then we will go spiritually to heaven, we do not have to strain our spirit up or down or sideways!

61 YET there is a need for us to lift up our physical eyes and hands to the starry heaven above. I mean when and if the spirit moves: not otherwise. For the things of the body are subject to those of the spirit, and are controlled thereby, and not the other way round.

An example of this may be found in the Ascension of our Lord: when the time appointed by his own will came for him to return to his Father in the body of his Manhood – he had never ceased, nor could cease being God – then in all his might, because God is spirit, the Manhood with its body followed in the one Person. And the outward manifestation of this was, most suitably, upwards.

This subjection of the body to the spirit can be seen after a fashion by those who are seeking to put the teaching of this book into action. For when a soul is determined to engage in this work, then, at the same time (and the contemplative does not notice it) his body, which perhaps before he began tended to stoop because this was easier, now through the spirit holds itself upright, and follows physically what has been done spiritually. All very fitting!

And because it is so fitting, man (who of all creatures has

1. Phil. 3:20

the most seemly body) is not made crooked, facing earth-wards, like all the other animals, but upright, facing heavenwards. Because the physical body should reflect the likeness of the spiritual soul, which should be upright spiritually and not crooked. Notice that I said 'upright spiritually', and not 'physically': how shall a soul which by nature is without a body be strained upright physically? It cannot be done.

So take care not to interpret physically what is intended spiritually, even though material expressions are used, like 'up, down, in, out, behind, before, this side, that side'. The most spiritual thing imaginable, if we are to speak of it at all – and speech is a physical action of the tongue, which is part of our body – must always be spoken of in physical words. But what of it? Are we therefore to understand it physically? Indeed not, but spiritually.

62 IN order that you may understand more easily when physical words, spoken by the tongue, are meant to be taken spiritually, I plan to explain to you the spiritual significance of some of the words that are used in connexion with the spiritual life. You will then know clearly and unmistakably when your spiritual work is inferior to you, and exterior; when it is interior and, as it were, on your level; and when it is superior to you, and inferior only to God.

Everything physical is external to your soul, and inferior to it in the natural order. Sun and moon and stars may all be above your physical body, but they are beneath your soul.

Angels and souls, however strong and beautiful they may be by grace and virtue, and superior indeed in purity, are nevertheless on the same level as yourself in the natural order.

Your soul has within itself, as part of the natural order, these faculties: the three major ones of *Mind* (which includes *Memory*), *Reason*, and *Will*, and two minor ones, *Imagination* and *Sensuality*.

There is nothing higher than yourself in the natural order, save God alone.

Whenever you come across the word 'yourself' in books on the spiritual life, it is your soul that is meant, and not your body.

According to the object on which your spiritual faculties are engaged, the work and quality of what you are doing is assessed, whether it is inferior, interior, or superior to you.

63 THE faculty of *Mind*, generally speaking, does no work by itself, whereas Reason and Will, like Imagination and Sensuality, are faculties that do. All these four faculties are held and embraced by mind. In no other sense than in this comprehensiveness can mind be said to work. I call some of the spiritual faculties major, some minor. Not because you can analyse the soul into parts, for that is impossible, but because these things with which they work can be analysed, some as major (e.g., all spiritual things) and some as minor (e.g. all material things). The two major faculties, reason and will, work on their own in all spiritual matters without the help of the other minor faculties. These latter however (imagination and sensuality), work in all forms of animal and physical life, whether reason and will are present or not. They are physical activities, and work with the physical senses. But by them alone, without the assistance of reason and will, a soul would never come

to know the moral and other qualities of physical creation, nor the reason for their existence, and why they do the things they do.

It is for this reason that we call reason and will major faculties, because they function entirely spiritually quite independently of material things. Imagination and sensuality are minor, because they work in the body with the bodily instruments, which are our five senses. Mind is called a major faculty because it spiritually embraces in itself not only all the other faculties, but also those things through which they work. Let me demonstrate.

64 REASON is the faculty by which we distinguish evil from good, bad from worse, good from better, worse from worst, better from best. Before man sinned his reason presumably would have done all this by light of nature. But now it is so blinded by original sin that it cannot do so unless it is enlightened by grace. Both reason itself, and the means by which it works, are included and stored in the mind.

Will is the faculty by which we choose good after it has been approved by reason, and by which we love God, desire God, and, ultimately, with complete satisfaction and consent, dwell in God. Before man sinned his will could not go wrong in its choice, its love or any of the things it did, because, then, it was able by nature to understand each thing as it really was. But it cannot do this now unless it is anointed with grace. Often now, because of the infection of original sin, it assesses a thing as good which in reality is bad, and has only the appearance of good. Both the will, and what it wills, the mind includes and enfolds within itself.

65 *IMAGINATION* is the faculty by which we can picture anything, past as well as present. Both it, and the means by which it works, are contained in the mind. Before man sinned, imagination was so obedient to its master, reason, that it never pictured anything that was perverted or fantastic, physically or spiritually; but not so now. For if it is not restrained by the light of grace in the reason, it will never cease, waking or sleeping, to suggest diverse and perverted ideas about the world around us, or some hallucination, which, after all, is only a spiritual idea conceived in material terms, or a material one conceived in spiritual. And this is always counterfeit and false, and akin to error.

This disobedience of the imagination can be clearly seen in the prayers of those who have been recently converted from the world to the life of devotion. For until the time comes when their imagination is, by and large, controlled by the light of grace in their reason – as happens after constant meditation on spiritual things, such as their own wretchedness, the Passion and kindness of our Lord, and so forth – they cannot overcome the amazing variety of thoughts, hallucinations, and pictures projected into and printed on their minds by their fertile imagination. And this disobedience is the outcome of original sin.

66 *SENSUALITY* is the faculty of our soul which affects and controls all our bodily reactions, and through which we know and experience the physical creation, both pleasant and unpleasant. It has two functions, one which looks after our physical needs, and one which provides for our physical appetites. It is the one and the same faculty that will grumble when the body is lacking essential requirements,

yet when the need is met, will move it to take more than it requires to maintain and further our desires. It grumbles when its likes are not met, and it is highly delighted when they are. It grumbles in the presence of what it dislikes, and is highly pleased when it is gone. This faculty and the means by which it works are included in the mind.

Before man sinned, sensuality was so obedient to will, its master as it were, that it never led it into perverted physical pleasure or pain, or any pretended spiritual pleasure or pain, induced by the enemy of souls into our earthly minds. But it is not so now. Unless it is ruled by grace in the will, so that it is prepared to suffer humbly and wholly the consequences of original sin (which it feels when it is deprived of its wonted pleasures, and can only have those irritating things that are so good for it!), and unless it will control both its strong desires when it has its wonted pleasures, and its greedy delight when the improving irritations are gone, it will wallow, like some pig in the mire, so wretchedly and wildly in all the wealth of the world, and the filth of the flesh, that the whole of its life will be animal and physical rather than human and spiritual.

67 My spiritual friend, to such degradation as you see here have we fallen through sin. Can we be surprised then that we are totally and easily deceived when we seek to understand the meaning of spiritual words and actions, especially if we do not yet know the faculties of our soul, and the way they work?

Whenever your mind is occupied with anything physical, however praiseworthy, you can be said to be 'beneath' yourself, and 'outside' your soul. And whenever you feel your mind engaged in the subtleties of the soul's faculties, and the way they work spiritually (such as vices or virtues, in yourself or in any other spiritual creature, and on the same natural level as yourself), in order that you might get to know yourself better, and to further your perfection, then you can be said to be 'within' yourself, and to have found your proper level. But whenever you feel your mind engaged, not in any physical or spiritual matter, but solely with God as he is (as the working out of the teaching of this book would prove) then you can be said to be 'above' yourself, and 'beneath' God.

Certainly you are above yourself, because you have succeeded in reaching by grace what you could not achieve by nature. And that is that you are united with God, in spirit, in love, and in harmony of will. You are beneath God, of course; for though in a manner of speaking you and God could be said at this time not to be two spiritually but one – so that you or whoever it is that perfectly contemplates may, because of this unity, truthfully be called 'a God' as the Bible says[1] – you are nonetheless beneath God. For he is God by nature and without beginning; and you once were nothing at all. And when afterwards you, by his power and love, were made something, you by your deliberate act of will made yourself less than nothing. And it is only by his wholly undeserved mercy that you are made a god by grace, inseparably united to him in spirit, here and hereafter in the bliss of heaven, world without end! So though you may be wholly one with him in grace, you are still infinitely beneath him in nature.

My spiritual friend, now you may understand a little how it is that a man who does not know how the faculties of his soul operate, or what they are, may very easily be deceived as to the meaning of words written with spiritual intent. And you may see, too, something of the reason why

1. John 10:34.

I dare not openly tell you to show your longing to God, but rather suggest that as in a child's game you do your best to conceal it. I do it because I am genuinely afraid that you might understand physically what is intended spiritually.

68 AND so it is that where another man might tell you to withdraw all your powers and thought within yourself, and worship God there – and he would be saying what was absolutely right and true – I do not care to do so, because of my fear of a wrong and physical interpretation of what is said. But what I will say is this: See that in no sense you withdraw into yourself. And, briefly, I do not want you to be outside or above, behind or beside yourself either!

'Well,' you will say, 'where am I to be? Nowhere, according to you!' And you will be quite right! 'Nowhere' is where I want you! Why, when you are 'nowhere' physically, you are 'everywhere' spiritually. Make it your business then to see that your spirit is tied to nothing physical, and you will find that wherever that thing is that you are giving your mind to, there you are too in spirit, just as surely as your body is where you are bodily! And, though your natural mind can now find 'nothing' to feed on, for it thinks you are doing no thing, go on doing this no thing, and do it for the love of God. Therefore, do not give up but work vigorously on that nothing, with vigilant longing and will to have God, whom no man can know. For I tell you truly that I would much rather be nowhere physically, wrestling with that obscure nothing, than I would be some great potentate who whenever I wanted could be anywhere I liked, and enjoy everything as if it were my own.

Let go this 'everywhere' and this 'everything' in

exchange for this 'nowhere' and this 'nothing'. Never mind if you cannot fathom this nothing, for I love it surely so much the better. It is so worthwhile in itself that no thinking about it will do it justice. One can feel this nothing more easily than see it, for it is completely dark and hidden to those who have only just begun to look at it. Yet, to speak more accurately, it is overwhelming spiritual light that blinds the soul that is experiencing it, rather than actual darkness or the absence of physical light. Who is it then who is calling it 'nothing'? Our outer self, to be sure, not our inner. Our inner self calls it 'All', for through it he is learning the secret of all things, physical and spiritual alike, without having to consider every single one separately on its own.

69 WHEN a man is experiencing in his spirit this nothing in its nowhere, he will find that his outlook undergoes the most surprising changes. As the soul begins to look at it, he finds that all his past sins, spiritual and physical, which he has committed from the day he was born are secretly and sombrely depicted on it. They meet his gaze at every turn, until at last after much hard work, many heartfelt sighs and many bitter tears he has virtually washed them all away.

At times in this spiritual struggle he thinks he might as well be looking at hell for the despair he feels of ever reaching perfection and peace out of all this suffering. Many come as far as this on their spiritual journey, but because their suffering is great and they get no comfort, they go back to the consideration of worldly things. They look for physical and external comfort to compensate for the missing and so far undeserved, spiritual comfort, which as a matter of fact they would have got if they had persevered.

For he that perseveres does at times feel comfort and have some hope of perfection, for he begins to feel, and indeed to see, that many of his past sins are by grace in process of being rubbed away. Though he still has to suffer, he now believes his suffering will one day come to an end, for it is all the time getting less and less. So he now begins to call it not 'hell' but 'purgatory'. At times he can find no particular sin written there, though he still thinks of sin in terms of a 'lump', which he does not analyse but knows to be himself. Then it may be called the foundation and painful result of original sin. At times he believes it to be paradise or heaven, because of the varied and wonderful delights, comforts, joys and blessed virtues he finds there. At times he believes it to be God, such is the peace and rest he finds.

Yes, let him think what he will; he will always find that a cloud of unknowing is between him and God.

70 WORK hard and with all speed in this nothing and this nowhere, and put on one side your outward physical ways of knowing and going about things, for I can truly tell you that this sort of work cannot be understood by such means.

With your eyes you can only understand a thing by its appearance; whether it is long or broad or small or large or round or square or coloured. With your ears you understand by noise or sound; with your nose by the stench or scent; with your taste whether it is sour or sweet, salt or fresh, bitter or pleasant; with your touch whether it is hot or cold, hard or soft, blunt or sharp.

But God and spiritual things have none of these varied

attributes. Therefore leave all outer knowledge gained through the senses; do not work with the senses at all, either objectively or subjectively. For if those who mean to become contemplatives, spiritual and inward looking, reckon they ought to hear, smell, see, taste, or feel spiritual things in external visions or in the depth of their being, they are seriously misled, and are working against the natural order of things. For the natural order is that by the senses we should gain our knowledge of the outward, material world, but not thereby acquire our knowledge of things spiritual. I mean, of course, by what the senses do. But by recognizing their limitations we may acquire such knowledge. For example, when we hear or read of certain things, and realize that our natural understanding cannot properly describe what they are, then we may be quite sure that those things are spiritual and not physical.

It happens in the same way spiritually, when within our hearts we strive to know God himself. For even if a man is deeply versed in the understanding and knowledge of all spiritual things ever created, he can never by such understanding come to know an uncreated spiritual thing ... which is none else than God! But by recognizing the reason for the limitation of his understanding, he may. Because the thing that limits his understanding is God, himself alone. That is why St Dionysius said, 'the most godlike knowledge of God is that which is known by unknowing.' Indeed, anyone who will read Dionysius's works will find that he clearly endorses all I have said, or will yet say, from beginning to end. Otherwise I would not bother to quote him now, or any other authority either. There was a time when it was thought humility if a man said nothing that was original without supporting it by Scripture and learned quotations. Today the practice provides the occasion for parading one's ingenuity and erudition. It is not necessary for you, and therefore I don't do it. Let him who has the will to hear, hear what I say, and let him who is moved to believe, believe what I say: there is no alternative.

71 THERE are those who think that this matter of contemplation is so difficult and frightening that it cannot be accomplished without a great deal of very hard work beforehand, and that it only happens occasionally, and then only in a period of ecstasy. Let me answer these people as well as I can: it depends entirely on the will and good pleasure of God, and whether they are spiritually able to receive this grace of contemplation, and the working of the Spirit.

For undoubtedly there are some who cannot attain this state without long and strenuous spiritual preparation, and who even so experience it in its fulness but rarely, and in response to a special call of our Lord – we would call this special call 'ecstatic'.

On the other hand there are some who by grace are so sensitive spiritually and so at home with God in this grace of contemplation that they may have it when they like and under normal spiritual working conditions, whether they are sitting, walking, standing, kneeling. And at these times they are in full control of their faculties, both physical and spiritual, and can use them if they wish, admittedly not without some difficulty, yet without great difficulty. We have an example of the first kind in Moses, and of the second in Aaron, the priest of the Temple. For the grace of contemplation is prefigured in the Old Law by the Ark of the Covenant, and contemplatives by those who had to look after the Ark, as the story will show. This grace and this work can appropriately be likened to that Ark, for just as the Ark contained all the jewels and relics of the temple, so our little love concentrated on this cloud of unknowing holds within itself all the virtues of a man's soul – and the soul is the spiritual temple of God.

Before Moses could see the ark and learn how it was to be made, he had to climb with long and toilsome effort to the top of the mountain, and remain there and work in a cloud for six days, and wait till on the seventh day our Lord condescended to show him the way in which the Ark should be made.[1] Moses's long and strenuous efforts and his delayed vision symbolize those who cannot reach the full height of this spiritual work without such preliminary effort and toil; even then the full experience is but seldom, and dependent upon God's condescension.

Moses could only 'see' on rare occasions, and then after much hard work, but Aaron on the other hand, by virtue of his office, had it in his power to see God in the temple behind the veil as often as he liked to go in. Aaron symbolizes all those I have just mentioned who by their spiritual wisdom and assisted by grace may achieve perfect contemplation whenever they like.

72 You can see by all this that the man who may only attain and experience perfect contemplation as the result of great effort, and then but seldom, may easily be quite wrong if he speaks or thinks or judges by his own experience, believing that men can only achieve it rarely, and after great effort. Similarly, the man who can achieve it whenever he likes may be quite wrong if he judges others by his own standards, and says that they too can have it when they will. Let it be? On the contrary, he really must

1. Ex. 25.

not be allowed to think this! For if and when God pleases, it may well be that those who achieve it at first but seldom, and only with great effort, shall afterwards have it when they will and as often as they like. Moses again is our example, who at first could only see the ark in a sort of way, rarely and after great effort on the mountain, but afterwards, as often as he liked, saw it in the valley.

73 THE three men that had most to do with this Old Testament Ark were Moses, Bezaleel, and Aaron. Moses learned in the mountain of our Lord how it should be made. Bezaleel did the work and made it in the valley, according to the pattern that was shown on the mountain. And Aaron kept it in the temple, to handle and see as often as he liked.

We can treat these three as symbols, and see in them three ways in which the grace of contemplation can benefit us. Sometimes the benefit is solely that of grace, and then we are like Moses who for all his climbing and effort on the mountain was seldom able to see it, and had the vision only when it pleased our Lord to grant it, and not as a reward for all his toil. Sometimes the benefit is the result of our own spiritual skill, helped by God's grace, and then we are like Bezaleel who was unable to see the ark before he had made it by his own efforts, but was assisted by the pattern showed to Moses in the mountain. And sometimes we benefit by other men's teaching, and then we are like Aaron who was in charge of the ark, and whose practice was to see and handle the ark that Bezaleel had previously fashioned and prepared whenever he pleased.

My spiritual friend, though I speak naïvely and ignorantly, and, wretch that I am, am unfit to teach anyone, I bear the office of Bezaleel, making and putting into your hands as it were some sort of spiritual ark. But you will have to work far better and more worthily than I if you are going to be an Aaron, by working at it constantly for your own sake – and mine! So go on, I beg you, for the love of God Almighty. And since we are both called by God to be contemplatives, I beg you for the love of God to make up on your part what is lacking on mine.

71. IF you think that this kind of contemplative work does not suit your temperament either physically or spiritually, then you may leave it, and, under sound spiritual direction, safely take another without blame.

Then I will have to ask you to excuse me, for my genuine intention was to help you as far as my simple knowledge would allow. Therefore read this book over two or three times, and the more often the better, for you will understand it better. Some sentence, perhaps, that was too hard for you at the first or second reading you will now think to be easy.

Yes, I feel it impossible to understand how any would-be contemplative can read or speak about this work, or hear it read or spoken of, without feeling immediately a very real concern for its outcome. So if you think it is doing you good, give God heartfelt thanks, and because you love him, pray for me. So go ahead. And I beg you for the love of God not to let anyone see this book unless he is in your judgement able to benefit from it in the sense that I described earlier when I said who should set out to be a contemplative, and when he should begin. If you do let any such see it, I beg you to insist that they give themselves plenty of time to digest it thoroughly. For there may be some matter at, say, the beginning or in the middle which is left in the air, and not fully explained in the context. If it is not dealt with there, it will be soon after, or by the end. If a man saw the matter only partially he might easily go wrong; therefore I beg you to do what I tell you. And if you think you need further information on any particular aspect, let me know what it is and what you yourself think about it, and I will do my simple best to put it right.

However, I do not want the loud-mouthed, or flatterers, or mock-modest, or busybodies, or talebearers, or cantankerous to see this book, for it never has been my intention to write all this for them. I would rather that they did not hear it ... and also those learned (and unlearned) people who are merely curious. Yes, even if they are good men judged from the active standpoint, all this will mean nothing to them.

75 NOT all those who read this book, or hear it read or spoken of, and as a result think it is a good and pleasant thing, are therefore called by God to engage in this work because of the pleasant sensation they get when they read it! This urge might well spring from a natural curiosity rather than from a call of grace.

But if they want to test the origin of their urge they can test it in this way if they like. In the first place let them see whether they have done everything possible in the way of preliminaries, preparing for it by cleansing their conscience according to the law of Holy Church and the advice of their director. So far so good. If they seek further assurance, let them inquire whether this urge constantly and habitually claims their attention more than other spiritual devotions.

And if they have come to believe that their conscience will not really approve anything they do, physical or spiritual, unless this secret little love which is fixed on the cloud of unknowing is the mainspring of their work spiritually, then it is a sign that they are being called to this work by God; otherwise not.

I am not saying that this urge goes on for ever and continually fills the thoughts of those called to contemplation. This is not so. For the actual feeling of urge often is withdrawn from the contemplative apprentice for a variety of reasons. Sometimes it is in order that he should not take it too much for granted, and think that in general it lies in his own power to have it as and when he likes. Such presumption is pride. Whenever the feeling of grace is withdrawn, pride is always the cause; not necessarily actual pride, but potential pride that would have arisen if the feeling had not been withdrawn. Because of this there are some young idiots who think God is their enemy, when in fact he is their best friend. Sometimes it is withheld because of their carelessness, and when this happens they subsequently experience a deep bitterness that eats into them like a canker. Sometimes our Lord delays the feeling of grace quite deliberately, because he wants by such delays to make it grow, and to be more highly appreciated; which is what happens when a thing that has been long lost is rediscovered. And here is one of the surest and most important signs a soul may have to know whether or not he is called to contemplation: if, when after a delay of this sort and a long inability to contemplate, it has come back suddenly, as it does, quite independently of him, he has a burning desire and a deeper passion for contemplation than ever before. Often, I fancy, his joy at its recovery far outweighs his distress at its loss! If this is so, it is surely a true and unmistakable sign that he has been called by God to become a contemplative, whatever he might have been formerly, or be still.

For it is not what you are or have been that God looks at with his merciful eyes, but what you would be. St Gregory asserts that 'all holy desires grow by delays; and if they fade because of these delays then they were never holy desires.' If a man feels less and less joy at new discoveries and the unexpected upsurge of his old and deliberate desires for good, then those desires never were holy. St Augustine is speaking of this holy desire when he says that 'the life of a good Christian consists of nothing else but holy desire'.

Farewell, spiritual friend, with God's blessing and mine upon you! I pray Almighty God that true peace, sound counsel, and his own spiritual comfort and abundant grace may ever be with you and all his earthly lovers.

AMEN

INTRODUCTION TO THE
EPISTLE OF PRIVY COUNSEL

Authorship

This little book claims to have been written by the author of *The Cloud of Unknowing*, and it names two other tracts from the same pen.[1] There is no reason to dispute this claim. Like *The Cloud* it is addressed to a particular but unnamed person.

Date

Since it is not known when *The Cloud* was written (1370ish is likely) it is not possible to date this work. It is generally believed to have been written some years later. It has all the signs of greater maturity; the pace is slower, some of the sparkle has gone, and the writing is more sober, but the message is the same, and many of the issues dealt with in *The Cloud* are found here, handled with authority and in more detail than in the earlier work. There are similar flashes of humour, mock-modest self-depreciation, and delight in debunking the high-brow. Linguistically, too, the style, rhythm, and language are similar, and there is the same skill in setting out profound themes in deceptively simple terms.

But the most plausible argument for a later date is the noticeable advance, both intellectually and spiritually, of the book's recipient. He can now cope with quotations from the Vulgate – though the Latin is always thoughtfully translated – and he is expected to follow closely-reasoned

1. *The Epistle of Prayer* and *Mystical Teaching*.

argument based primarily on experience and supported by Scripture. To describe his mystical state in the terms of two centuries later, he seems to have passed from the 'dark night of the senses' into the 'dark night of the spirit'.

A gap, then, of some years between *The Cloud* and *Privy Counsel* seems to be indicated, and it could be that the offer made in Chapter 74 of the former has been taken up, and *Privy Counsel* and some, if not all, of the cognate works here translated, are the outcome.

Leading Ideas

Whether or not the suggestion in the preceding paragraph is likely, there is no doubt that the stress on the total abandonment of the soul to God was worrying the reader, and that he was seeking advice. *Privy Counsel* is at pains to explain and insist on 'the naked intent' needed to reach God; 'naked' in the sense that words and thoughts are irrelevant and normally a hindrance in an advanced state of prayer, and 'intent' in the demand that the soul means to have God at all cost, though on God's terms, of course, and not its own. This is the basic Christian teaching that prayer is fundamentally an act of will, and not a pious or enjoyable feeling.

So the writer argues, cogently and forcefully, for wordless, even mindless, prayer as a concomitant of contemplation, and this runs like a master theme throughout the whole treatise. This simple *remise à Dieu* is the recognition, in fact as well as in theory, that the self depends for its being on God who is himself both its cause and its sustainer. Contemplation is in essence the experience that God is our very being, all other consciousness having been excluded, and the 'naked intent' is the utter determination of the soul to appropriate this fact. In the words of the author what matters is 'not *what* thi-self is, bot *that* thi-self is'. What one thinks or feels about God or his creation (including oneself) is unimportant: the essential thing is that all 'self' consciousness should be lost in 'God' consciousness. The most bitter sorrow a soul can have is to know that it stands out from, and therefore against, God. Until its existence ('that he is') is united to Reality ('he that is') it is bereft indeed.

But this is no Buddhist 'annihilation' or Zen 'satori'. Though the soul is seeking to divest itself of its 'self', offering it up to God in love (for 'this is the trewe condicion of a parfite lover'), yet in fact it does not 'coveit for to un-be', but to be rid of the conscious knowledge of its being, 'until,' as Keble would say, 'in the ocean of thy love we lose ourselves'.

This emphasis on love, both God's for us, and ours for him, tends to distinguish Christian from other forms of mysticism. It is found throughout the writings of *The Cloud* family. On the whole it is a pretty earthy kind of love, being the spiritual sublimation of the love that unites the sexes.

The New Testament uses three words for which the English translation is 'love'. *Agapē* means the unemotional kind of love which is primarily a matter of mind and will: it is the great word for love, being used more than 250 times; *philia* is the love that cherishes; and *storgē* represents family affection. There is a fourth word, *erōs*, which is never used by New Testament writers because of the degenerate and corrupt significance that then attached to it. It means sexual love. It is this word that Christian mysticism has rescued and redeemed. And now the word bears this fourfold meaning, and alongside the New Testament usage there is associated human, erotic love, purged of all beastliness, but recognizable, and symbolic of the warm, embracing, possessing love of God for the soul who, as it yields to him its all, loses all awareness of selfhood in the wonder of union.

The soul's knowledge of God in this union is, not surprisingly, quite indescribable, so far is it beyond and different from human genius. All that can be said can only be said *about* it: the experience itself is incommunicable. The awareness that such a happening might occur is granted to the one whose soul has been purged from sin, and who feels in his heart that this is his calling of God, a call which he has checked with his director and Scripture. The proof of its genuineness depends on two signs: an interior one, the inescapable and persistent desire for God himself, and not for his things; and an outer sign, the unquenchable pleasure that haunts and thrills whenever the subject is mentioned, and which refuses to be quietened. Yet it is not for this sense of fulfilment that the soul's 'naked intent' reaches out. It wants, and means, God, and God in his own way and not the soul's.

Many of the other *Cloud* themes are echoed in *Privy Counsel*, such as the hard work that contemplation involves, the darkness of the intellect, the need for the grace of Jesus, the distinction between active and contemplative, and much else. But everything is subsidiary to the main emphasis on the utter determination to have God. Round that pivot the writing revolves. This is Christian mysticism at its best. There is nothing 'instant' about it, and very little emotion. It demands much solid grind and much discipline, but in God's time one 'is caught up into Paradise, and hears unspeakable words, not lawful' (or possible) 'to utter.'

THE EPISTLE OF
PRIVY COUNSEL

(THE BOOK OF PRIVE COUNSELING)

PROLOGUE

My friend in God,

If I understand your mind aright, as I think I do, I am going to speak to you personally, and not to any of those who may chance to overhear. Were I writing for all and sundry I would write in general terms. But since I am now writing specially for you I am going to say only such things as I think apply to your particular case. Should anyone else be in like state and find what I write helpful, so much the better; I shall be pleased. All the same I shall be concentrating on what seems to me to be your inner problem. And so I say to you, representative of all like minded, this:

MY FRIEND IN GOD

1 When you have reached the state of recollection, do
not worry about the next step, but just stop thinking your
'good' thoughts as well as your 'bad' ones. Do not pray
with words unless you feel you have to, and even then, if
you do, do not bother about their being many or few. Nor
are you to pay any attention to their meaning, whatever
it is you are praying, whether it is a collect, psalm, hymn,
antiphon, or what, whether you are interceding generally
or specifically, praying internally and mentally, or outwardly and vocally. See that nothing occupies your
thoughts except an utter determination[1] to reach out to
God: no special thought about what he is, or how he works,
but only that he is as he is. Let him be himself, please, and
nothing else. You are not to go probing into him with your
smart and subtle ideas. That belief must be your foundation.

This utter determination, firmly based as it is on true
belief, must be the simple recognition and blind acceptance
of your own existence, and no more than this, either intellectually or emotionally. It is as if you were saying to
God, 'What I am, Lord, I offer you. I am not thinking of
you in any particular way, except that you are as you are,
no more and no less'.

That humble and intellectual darkness must be reflected
in all your thinking. I would say more: you are not to
think about yourself any more than you do about God,
so that you are one with him in spirit – not however at the
cost of mental disintegration! For he is your being, and

1. Literally 'naked intent'.

what you are you are in him, not merely because of this fact, but because in you he is both the cause and the reason for your existence. Therefore at this stage you are to think of God in the same way that you think of yourself, and of yourself as you do of God, namely that he is as he is, and that you are as you are. In this way your thinking will not be dissipated or confused but unified in him who is all; never forgetting, of course, this difference: that he is your being, and not you his.

For though it is true that all things have their being in him who is their cause and their explanation, and that he is in them for that very reason, it is only he in himself who is his own cause and being. Just as nothing can exist without him, so he too cannot exist without himself. He is his own existence and everything else's. He alone is distinct from all else, in that he is the being of himself and everything. Too, he is one in all things, and all are one in him, for all have their being in him who is the being of all. Like this your thinking and your love will be indissolubly united to him by his grace, and all those odd queries about the abstruse characteristics of your unseen self, or God's, will be put well away. Your thinking will be utterly simple, your affection unspoiled, and you yourself in all your basic poverty by his gracious touch will be secretly nourished by himself, just as he is. Unseen and incomplete it may be – it has to be so in this life – but in this way your longing and your desire will be stimulated.

Look up cheerfully and tell your Lord, either aloud or in your heart, 'What I am, Lord, I offer you, for it is yourself'. And keep in mind, simply, plainly, and unashamedly, that you are as you are, and that there is no need to inquire more closely.

This is not a very difficult thing to do, however stupid one might be – or so it seems to me. Sometimes I have to smile, albeit ruefully, when people say to my surprise (and they are not the simple and illiterate, but those who are learned and extremely clever) that what I write to you and others is so difficult and technical, so subtle and illusive, that it can hardly be understood by a theologian however erudite, or by any man or woman however intelligent. At least this is what they say. I invariably answer that nowadays it is not just a handful but nearly everyone – there may possibly be the odd exception among the 'specially chosen of God' – who is blinded by subtle scholarship, theological or natural. And this is a cause for deep regret and something to be rejected (in mercy, of course), and severely rebuked by God and his lovers. For the result is that through their blindness and sophistication people have no more insight and understanding of this simple exercise than the child at his ABC has of the knowledge of the greatest scholar in the university – if indeed as much. Yet in truth it is this simple exercise that can unite the soul of the most uncouth man alive to God in love and humility and perfect charity.

Because they are blind they mistakenly call this simple teaching 'intellectual subtlety', whereas if only they were to look at it properly they would find it to be a straightforward, easy lesson for simple people. For the only man I can think of who would be too stupid or ignorant for this would be the man who was incapable of recognizing that he existed: ignorant not of *what* he is, so much as *that* he is. Clearly it is natural for the most ignorant cow or unintelligent animal (can we or can we not say that one creature is more stupid and unintelligent than another?) to be aware of its own existence. Then it is much more likely that man, who alone of the animal kingdom has been endowed with reason, should recognize his own existence!

So you must get down to the basic essentials of thought

(some people, remember, consider it the most sophisticated!) and think of yourself in the simplest way (again, some think it is the wisest), not *what* you are, but *that* you are. Why, for you to be able to think *what* you are, you with all your characteristics and capacities, calls for a great deal of skill and knowledge and insight, and much shrewd inquiry into your natural intelligence. You have done this at some time already with the help of God's grace and now you know, at least in part and as much as is good for you, what you are: a human being by nature, and a filthy stinking wretch by sin. How well you know it! Perhaps, indeed, only too well all the filth that goes along with the wretch. Shame! Let go of it, I beg you. Don't keep stirring it up: the stench is frightful. But to know *that* one exists is possible for anyone, however ignorant or uncouth he may be; it does not call for any great knowledge or aptitude.

2 So please do no more in this matter than realize quite simply that you are as you are, foul and wretched though you be. I am taking it for granted of course that you have been duly absolved of your sins, particular and general, according to the true teaching of Holy Church. Otherwise neither you nor anyone else would have the nerve to engage in this work: at least not with my consent. But if you feel you have done all you should, then you can start. Even if you still believe yourself to be so vile and wretched that you are a burden to yourself and do not know what course to follow, just do what I am going to tell you.

Take good, gracious God just as he is, and without further ado lay him on your sick self just as you are, for all the world as if he were a poultice! Or to put it in other words, lift up your sick self just as you are, and through your longing strive to touch good, gracious God just as he is. Touching him is eternal health, which is the point of the story of the woman in the Gospel who said, *Si tetigero vel fimbriam vestimenti ejus, salva ero*,[1] 'If I touch but the hem of his garment I shall be whole'. Much more will you be 'made whole' of your sickness through this marvellous heavenly touch. For you are touching his very being, his own dear self. Stand up then like a man, and apply the remedy. Lift that sick self of yours, just as it is, up to gracious God, just as he is. Don't give a thought, however ingenious, to any or all of your own qualities, or God's, whether those attributes are pure or wretched, grace-given or natural, divine or human. All that matters now is that this unseeing awareness of your basic self should be carried up with glad, vigorous love and, by the grace of the Holy Spirit, united with the precious being of God, just as he is in himself, no more and no less.

Your wayward curiosity can find nothing solid to hold on to in a happening of this sort, and so it grumbles and tells you to stop doing it and do something 'useful' in the curious way people understand it – for it seems to these that what you are doing is not at all important: they don't know the first thing about it! I would therefore love it all the more, for this is a sign that it is much more worthwhile than anything they are doing. And why indeed should I not like it all the more, particularly when there is nothing for me to do, nothing for my fancy and imagination to work out, physically or spiritually? Nothing brings me so near to God, and so far from the world as this simple straightforward experience, this surrender of my basic self.

So although your mind can find nothing to feed on, and therefore wants you to do something else, you are not

1. Mark 5:28, Luke 8:44.

to give up merely because it tells you to; you are to be its master. You are not to go back to feeding it, however cross it gets. Once you allow it to explore the various (and odd) theories about your faculties or your existence you are beginning to go backwards and feed it. Such meditations, good and helpful though they be, when they are preferred to this simple straightforward experience, this surrender of yourself, break up and destroy that perfect union which theoretically ought to exist between God and the soul. So keep a firm grip on this spiritual, fundamental principle, which is your own existence. On no account go back to the old ways, even when they seem good and holy and your mind is inclining thereto.

3 FOLLOW the advice and teaching that Solomon gave his son, *Honora Dominum de tua substantia, et de primiciis frugum tuarum da pauperibus, et inplebuntur horrea tua saturitate et vino torcularia redundabunt,*[1] 'Honour the Lord with your wealth, and with the first fruits of all your increase give to the poor; so will your barns be filled with plenty, and your vats burst with new wine'. These are Solomon's actual words, but he would have you understand them spiritually in the sense which I am now about to give on his behalf:

'My friend in God, make certain you have stopped theorizing with your natural powers; make sure too that you are worshipping God with your whole being, offering him simply and completely your whole self, all you are and what you are. And you must do this in a general sense rather than a particular: in other words, without considering in detail what it is you are. In this way your vision of

1. Proverbs 3:9–10.

God will not fade, nor your experience of him go sour, in the sense that it would lessen your union with God in the purity of your spirit. And you are to "feed the poor" with your "first fruits"; in other words those major spiritual and physical faculties you have grown up with from the moment you were created to this very day.'

I call *fruits* all those gifts of nature and grace God has given you. With them you are expected to feed and to cherish your brothers and sisters, natural and spiritual, as you do yourself. The first of these gifts I call your *first fruits*. In every creature this is quite simply its existence. For though it is true that what you are is inseparably bound up with the fact that you are, yet because the one depends on the other this latter may be quite properly called the first of your gifts, for such indeed it is. So your first fruit is the simple fact of your existence. If you analyse the way you look at the complex gifts and splendid characteristics which make up man (who is the noblest of all created things) you will always find that however you look at them the fundamental and final thing is the sheer fact that you exist. It is as though you were saying to yourself whenever you were engaged in meditation and stimulating your love and praise for the Lord God (who not only gave you existence but one of such a quality as your very gifts testify), 'I am; and I see and feel that I am; and not only that I am, but that I am moreover this thing and that, and so on and so forth'. For in this way you would be reckoning up every quality that makes you what you are. And summing it all up, you would say, 'What I am, and how I am, by nature and by grace, I have received from you, Lord. It is you yourself. I offer all of it to you, in the first instance for your praise, but also to help my fellow Christians and myself.' Like this you can see that first and foremost, before there is any contemplating, the basic, plain fact is your awareness that you exist, even if you only perceive it vaguely. So it is your existence alone that is the first of your fruits.

But though it is the first of your fruits and everything else depends on it, it is not important at this present juncture to link up your consideration of it with any particular aspect of your fruits, as I call them, and on which you have spent so much energy. It is sufficient now that you should worship God as wholeheartedly as possible, simply offering up to him your existence, your first fruits, in an unceasing sacrifice of praise, for yourself and everything else, as charity demands. And you do all this, quite independently of any particular reflection which may happen to spring from the fact that you exist, and that others do too; even when by such consideration you might help the needy, or further the well-being, or increase the perfection of yourself or someone else. Let it be: in this case it does not really help. This blind, general sort of contemplation helps your need, your well-being, and your progress towards perfection in purity of spirit (and not only yours) more than any special consideration you may make, be it never so holy.

The truth of this is attested by Scripture, by Christ's example, and by common sense. All men were lost in Adam, for he fell from the love which bound him to God. All men, who by their good works done according to their lights show they want to be saved, can only be saved now and hereafter by the passion of Christ, who offered himself as the true sacrifice. His sacrifice was made for all men in general, and not for some individuals in particular: it was, and is, 'common' and available to all. So he, truly and perfectly sacrificing himself for the good of all, does all that is possible to him to unite men with God as effectively as he himself is united to him.

'Greater love has no man than this'[1] if he sacrifices himself for all his brothers and sisters, spiritual and natural. For as the soul is more important than the body, so the uniting of the soul to God, its life, by the heavenly food of love, is better than the uniting of the body to the soul, its life, by earthly food. This latter is, of course, a good thing to do for its own sake, but without the other it is ever incomplete. Both together are better, but best of all is the first. The uniting of soul and body as such will never merit salvation, but the other union by itself, even if all else fails, not only deserves salvation, but leads on to the greatest perfection.

4 IF you are going to grow more perfect there is no need to feed your mind by thinking about your different attributes, and thereby to nourish your affection with lovely and loving feelings about God and spiritual things. Nor is there need to fill your understanding with that spiritual wisdom which is based on holy meditations seeking to know God. For if, as is possible by grace, you will concentrate on the fundamental thing about yourself, and offer God that naked, unseeing awareness of your own existence (your 'first fruits', remember) you can be quite sure that the second part of Solomon's lesson will be fulfilled as completely as he promised. And this will happen without all that busy, fussy, spiritual canvassing of those qualities that make up your being – and God's being too.

For you must be absolutely clear that in this matter you are not considering the attributes of God's being any more than your own. For in terms of the eternity which is God there is no description, experience, or consideration as good

1. John 15:13.

as or better than that which is had, seen, and known in the blind, loving consideration of this word *is*. For if you say *good*, or *fair Lord*, *sweet*, *merciful*, or *righteous*, *wise* or *omniscient*, *mighty* or *almighty* Lord, or that he is *knowledge* or *wisdom*, *power* or *strength*, *love* or *charity* – whatever it is you are wanting to say about God, you will find it all summed up and contained in this little word *is*. Mention every one of them, and you have said nothing extra; say nothing at all, and you do not diminish it. Therefore be as 'blind' in your loving contemplation of God's being as you are in the naked contemplation of your own, and don't go searching after special qualities peculiar to him – or to you. Put speculation firmly aside, and worship God with all you have got. All-that-you-are-as-you-are worshipping all-that-he-is-as-he-is. For only he, and he completely, is his own blessed being – and yours too.

In this way (and it really is marvellous!) you will be worshipping God in union with himself, for what you are you have through him and, indeed, it is himself. Though you had beginning when your substance was created (for there was a time when you did not exist) yet in him your being has existed from eternity, without beginning and without ending just as he too is in himself. And so I constantly proclaim this one thing, 'Worship God with your substance,[1] and with your first fruits bless mankind. Then will your barns be completely filled.' Which means `that your spiritual affection will be filled to the brim with love and from the virtue of your life in God, the foundation of your purity of heart'.

'And your vats burst with wine'. In other words those interior, spiritual faculties of yours (which you squeeze and strain with your speculations which pry into God and

1. 'Substance': a *double entendre* here. 'Belonging' (all that you have) and 'being' (what you are).

yourself, his characteristics and your own) 'shall then burst with wine'. In the Bible the mystical and true significance of *wine* is the spiritual wisdom that is gained through real contemplation and a deep experience of God.

All this happens suddenly, sweetly, and by grace, with no help or assistance on your part. It is done by ministering angels, and is the result of this blind exercise of love. For the angels know how to serve it specially, just as a maid serves her mistress.

5 THAT wise man, Solomon, warmly recommends this simple and delightful exercise. Basically it is the supreme Wisdom of God coming down graciously into a man's soul, joining it in union to himself in simplicity and prudence. Solomon exclaims, *Beatus homo qui invenit sapientiam et qui affluit prudentia. Melior est acquisitio ejus negotiatione auri et argenti. Primi et purissimi fructus ejus. Custodi, fili mi, legem atque consilium: et erit vita animae tuae et gratia faucibus tuis. Tunc ambulabis fiducialiter in via tua et pes tuus non inpinget. Si dormieris, non timebis; quiesces et suavis erit somnus tuus. Ne paveas repentino terrore, et irruentes tibi potentias impiorum, quia Dominus erit in latere tuo et custodiet pedem tuam ne capiaris.*[1] All of which adds up to this: he is a happy

---

1. Proverbs 3:13–14, 21–6.

The Jerusalem Bible thus translates:

Happy the man who discovers wisdom,
　　the man who gains discernment:
gaining her is more rewarding than silver,
　　more profitable than gold.

My son, hold to sound judgement and prudence,
　　do not let them out of your sight;

man who finds this unifying wisdom; who succeeds in his
spiritual exercises through this loving simplicity and spiritual insight; who offers up to God the blind awareness of
his own being; who puts far behind him all his scholarly
knowledge and questionings, intellectual and natural alike.
Getting hold of this spiritual wisdom by this simple exercise is better than getting gold or silver. By *gold* and *silver*
we understand those other forms of knowledge, natural or
spiritual, which we obtain through subtle speculation, or
the use of our natural faculties on things around us, or by
considering properties peculiar to God and his creation.
Why it should be better Solomon shows when he says
primi et purissimi fructus ejus, which means 'for its fruits are
best and purest'. No wonder, for the fruit of this exercise
is advanced spiritual wisdom, suddenly and freely thrown
up by the spirit from within itself; it is spontaneous and
completely real; it cannot be controlled, nor is it subject
to natural thought. For natural thought, be it never so
sensitive or holy, in comparison with this can only be called
'false and foolish fantasy, unreal and stupid'. In the full

---

they will prove the life of your soul,
  an ornament round your neck.
You will go on your way in safety,
  your feet will not stumble.
When you sit down you will not be afraid,
  when you lie down, sweet will be your sleep.
Have no fear of sudden terror
  or of assault from wicked men,
since Yahweh will be your guarantor,
  he will keep your steps from the snare.

The author's quotation is *almost* identical with the received text of
the Latin Vulgate. He has however transposed *auri* (gold) and *argenti*
(silver), and possibly as a result has regarded *primi et purissimi ejus*
fructus as nominative plural and therefore an independent phrase,
and not, as does the Vulgate, as genitive qualifying *auri*.

light of the spiritual sun it is as far from the real truth as
the darkness of a moonbeam on a foggy midwinter night
would be from the brightness of a sunbeam on midsummer
day!

'My son,' he says, 'keep this law and this counsel'. For
in it all the commandments and counsel of the Bible are
really and truly fulfilled, and with no special emphasis on
any particular one. The only reason why this is called a
'law' is that it contains completely within itself all the
branches and fruits of the law. If you look at it closely you
will see that its basis and power is nothing less than the
glorious gift of love, in which, as the apostle says, 'all the
law is fulfilled'.[1] *Plenitudo legis est dilectio*, 'The fulness of
the law is love'.

And if you keep it, says Solomon, this law of love and
this counsel of life will be 'life to your soul and grace to
your countenance'; the first inwardly in your tender love
to God, and the second outwardly in the truth of your
teaching, in your self-control, and in the way you live
among your fellow Christians. On these two, inner and
outer, 'hang all the law and the prophets,' as Christ
teaches. *In his enim duobus tota lex pendet et prophetae:
scilicet, dilectio Dei et proximi* [2]

So when you have been made perfect within and without, you will go forward in trust. God's grace will be your
foundation and guide on the spiritual way, lovingly lifting
up your being – naked and blind as it is – to God's blessed
being, beings which are one through grace, though different, of course, in nature.

And Solomon continues: 'And the foot of your love will

1. Romans 13:10.
2. Matthew 22:40. 'For on these two (commandments) hang all
the Law and the Prophets: namely, love of God and one's neigh-
bour'.

not stumble'; his meaning is that 'once you have shown through this spiritual activity that your spirit will persevere, then you are not going to be put off so easily, or held back by clever guesswork as happens in the early stages'. However it could also mean that 'the foot of your love will not stumble or trip over any idea, however fantastic, which results from guessing and speculating'. This is the only reason, as I have already pointed out, why in this exercise every speculation of the natural mind is to be utterly and completely rejected and forgotten. Then there will be no fear of fantasy or falsehood to foul the naked feeling of your blind being, or to draw you away from the real value of this exercise.

For if you think about anything in particular except your own bare, blind existence – and this, remember, is God's purpose and your own – then you are on the wrong track; you are back again at your speculating and guessing; and this distracts and separates you not only from God but from yourself as well. So take a firm grip on yourself as best you can, helped by grace and the wisdom that results from perseverance in this work.

For it is in this unseeing seeing of your bare existence which is now united to God that you will do all you have to do, as has been said: eating or drinking, sleeping or waking, walking or sitting, speaking or silence, resting or rising, standing or kneeling, running or riding, toiling or relaxing. Each day you are to offer this up to God as the most precious offering you can make. It is more important than anything you do, be it active or contemplative. It is what Solomon is saying in this passage, 'If you sleep' in this unseeing seeing from all the racket and machinations of the foul fiend, the false world, and the frail flesh 'you will not be afraid of any danger' or trick of the devil. For in this matter he is completely fogged and blinded, pained and ignorant, and he fumes to know what you are doing. Never mind, for 'you will rest quietly' in this loving union of God and your soul, and 'your sleep will be sweet'. It will provide spiritual food and inner strength to body as well as to soul. For, as Solomon goes on to say almost at once, *Universae carni sanitas est*,[1] 'It is health to all the weaknesses and ills of the flesh'. He is quite right. For since all sickness and corruption took hold of the flesh when the soul ceased this exercise, so all health will return when the soul bestirs itself to start again. And this can happen by the grace of Jesus, who is the real power behind it. But you can only hope to have this by Jesus' mercy and your loving concurrence. So as Solomon does in this passage I too pray that you will vigorously maintain this practice, and ever give him your glad and loving consent.

Et ne paveas repentino terrore et irruentes tibi potentias impiorum,[2] 'Do not be dismayed' by any uneasy fear though the Fiend come – and he will! – 'with sudden terror', pounding and battering the walls of the house where you sit; though he prompts one of his powerful allies to attack you suddenly and without warning. You can be sure that this will happen if you seriously mean business. In one or other of your five senses you will see, feel, smell, taste, or hear some strange thing, devil-concocted. His whole aim is to drag you down from the heights of this precious undertaking. So take great care of your heart at this testing time, and lean with eager trust on our Lord's love. *Quia Dominus erit in latere tuo, et custodiet pedem tuam ne capiaris*, 'Our Lord will be at your side,' ready and at hand to help, and 'he will keep your foot' (this means the love that takes you up to God) so that you will not be snared by the subtle

1. Proverbs 4:22.
2. Have no fear of sudden terror or of assault from wicked men. Proverbs 3:25.

tricks of your enemies (the Fiend and his followers, the
world, and your flesh). My friend, so does our Lord and
our Love powerfully, wisely, and kindly help, keep, and
defend those who utterly forsake all concern for themselves because they love and trust him.

6 BUT where are we to find such a soul, so surely
grounded in the Faith, so completely humble in its self-
denial, so lovingly led and nourished by love for our
Lord? A soul who really knows and experiences God's
omnipotence, his unsearchable wisdom, his glorious goodness? A soul who knows how God is one in all, and how
all exist in him, and realizes that it can never know true
humility or total abandonment until and unless it surrenders
in its love everything to him? It is only through this great
act of total self-denial, this genuine humility, this exalting
of God as its all in all in perfect charity, that the soul deserves to have God. Completely absorbed in the love of
God, and once and for all abandoning itself as less than
nothing (were that possible!) the soul experiences the
power and wisdom and goodness of God to sustain, keep,
and protect it from its enemies, both physical and spiritual.
And that, with no effort or hard work, no consideration
or self-love on its own part.

So let go those merely man-made objections, you souls
only half-humble! Don't go thinking that this humble and
complete surrender of all attempts to look after yourself –
which you believe to be the result of God's grace – means
you are putting God to the test, simply because you fancy
this is something you would not dare do on your own.
No, be satisfied with your own part, for it is sufficient to
save the souls of all in the active state. Leave contemplative

souls to look after themselves. Don't go brooding or worrying over what they say or do, even when you think they have gone much too far.

Shame! How much longer are you going to know about all this and yet give it no credence? I am meaning that very thing the Fathers of old wrote about and taught, the fruit and flower of the whole Bible. Otherwise it would seem that you are blind, unable to believe what you read and hear, or else are moved by some subconscious envy which will not allow so great a blessing to be given to your brothers if you do not have it yourself! It is good to be aware of this, for your enemy is subtle, out to make you trust more in your own reasoning powers than in the orthodoxy of the early Fathers, or in the work of grace, and the will of our Lord.

How often must you have read and heard, and from those who are holy, wise, and faithful, that as soon as Benjamin was born his mother, Rachel, died? Benjamin stands for 'contemplation', Rachel for 'reason'. Once a soul has experienced true contemplation (the result of this splendid act of self-abnegation and total response to God who is all) then man's reason dies, surely and really. Now if you have often read about this, not only from one or two writers, but from very many who are genuinely holy and worthy, why don't you believe it? And if you do believe it, how dare you criticize and cross-examine Benjamin's words and deeds? Benjamin represents all those who in the ecstasy of love are ravished beyond the scope of reason. As the prophet says *Ibi Beniamyn adulescentulus in mentis excessu*, 'There is Benjamin, a young child, in ecstasy'. So take good care you are not like those dreadful women who kill their children as soon as they are born! It is just as well to make sure that in your presumption you are not aiming your spear at the powerful purpose and will of our Lord, however confident you may be of your own ability. Your shortsightedness and lack of experience may bring him down at the very moment you think you are giving him support.

In the early days of the Church, when persecution was rife, all sorts of people suddenly experienced a wonderful touch of grace without any prior warning, so that craftsmen would at once throw down their tools, and schoolboys their books, and without more ado run to be martyred with the saints. If that was so then why cannot we believe that today in peaceful times God may, can, will, and indeed does, touch different souls just as suddenly with the gift of contemplation? I believe he is willing, through his great grace, to do just this in chosen souls. After all, ultimately he is going to be known for what he is, to the wonderment of the whole world. Such a soul, lovingly making itself nothing and exalting God as all in all, is not going to be overthrown by its foes, physical or spiritual. And that will happen through no effort or exertion of its own but solely through the grace and goodness of God. This is only what sanctified common sense would expect: that God should keep safe all who for love of him forsake themselves, indifferent to their own welfare. Small wonder then that they are marvellously kept, who are completely humble in their courageous, strong love.

As for him who dares not do this, or even opposes it, either it is the devil in his heart enticing him away from the loving trust he should have towards God, and the goodwill he should have towards his fellow Christians, or else he is not as perfectly humble as he ought to be. I assume, of course, that he is intending to be a real contemplative.

There is no need for you to be shy either of humbling yourself before our Lord, or even of sleeping in this unseeing seeing of God as he is, away from all the racket of this wicked world: away too from the deceitful devil and your own frail flesh. Our Lord is ready to help you and will 'keep your foot from being taken'.

This work can well be likened to a 'sleep'. For just as in sleep the use of our physical faculties is suspended so that the body may have its full rest and replenish its natural powers, so in this spiritual sleep the wayward questionings of our imagination, so undisciplined and fantastic, are fettered and made powerless. Now the blessed soul can sleep quietly and rest in the loving contemplation of God just as he is, and thereby nourish and reinforce its spiritual nature.

So keep a tight rein on your imagination when you offer up this naked, blind awareness of yourself to God. And make quite sure, as I am always saying, that it is naked, and not dolled up in some particular attribute of your being. For if you do 'clothe' it in some way – for example, with your own self-worthiness, or some other human or creaturely quality – then you will at once feed your imagination, and give it the opportunity and strength to drag you down to trivialities of every kind, chaotic beyond belief. Be on your guard against this trick, I beg you.

7 But now, perhaps, because you have been looking into the processes of your thinking, and because they have had no previous experience of this work, you are wondering about it all and are suspicious. It is not surprising; up to now you have been too sophisticated to know about such things. You are asking yourself, perhaps, how you can know whether this work pleases God or not; and, if it is enjoyable, how it can be as enjoyable as I say it is. My answer would be that your question is prompted by intellectual curiosity, which will not let you consent to this

work unless it can be justified by logical argument. I am not going to stop you. However, up to a point I shall make myself like you, and flatter your intellectual pride, so that subsequently you can become like me, and by following my advice set no limit to your humility!

For it is just as Saint Bernard says, 'Perfect humility knows no limits',[1] though you of course are setting limits to your humility by refusing to accept the advice of your spiritual director unless your intellect agrees with it. Now look: by this time you must realize that I am wanting to be your director! Indeed I do, and I intend to be so! Yet I believe it is love that is prompting me rather than any ability I am aware of, or any technical knowledge I may happen to possess, or any proficiency in this life. God correct what is amiss, for he knows it fully, I only in part.

But now that I am commending this exercise (I must make some concession to your intellectual pride!) I tell you for a fact that if a soul engaged in contemplation could put his experience into words all the theologians in Christendom would marvel at such wisdom. Yes indeed, and in comparison with it all their great learning would seem sheer folly. No wonder, then, that my rough earthy tongue is quite unable to describe its immense worthwhileness. God forbid that it should be distorted by the pathetic attempts of my carnal tongue! No, this must not happen; nor indeed will it – and God forbid that I should want otherwise. For everything that is said about it is not the thing itself, but is only *about* it. So now, if we cannot *speak* it, let us speak *about* it – to the confusion of all intellectual pride, and yours in particular! It is the only reason, or the occasion at least, for my writing at this time.

First of all I would ask what is meant by the 'perfection of man's soul', and what are the qualities that produce it?

1. *Liber de Praecepto et Dispensatione*, Chapter 6.

And on your behalf I would reply that such perfection is nothing but the union effected between God and the soul in perfect love. This perfection is fundamentally so fine and pure, so far above human understanding, that it cannot be known or seen as it really is. But where the characteristics of this perfection are in fact being seen, it is likely that the real thing is present. So we must know then what these characteristics are if we are to demonstrate the superiority of this spiritual exercise over every other.

The characteristics that make up perfection, and which every perfect soul must have, are the virtues. Now if you will seriously look at this work of contemplation going on in your soul, and at the property and nature of each virtue separately, you will find that each virtue is clearly and completely comprehended in it; and that, moreover, without our having to force it or distort it from its original purpose.

There is no need for me to be more specific, for you will find the virtues dealt with in some way in my other writings. For this work if it is rightly understood is the reverent love, 'the fruit separated from its tree', that I spoke of in my little *Epistle of Prayer*. This is the *Cloud of Unknowing*; this is that secret love springing from a pure spirit; this is the *Ark of the Covenant*; this is Dionysius' *Mystical Theology*, his wisdom and his dowry, his 'shining darkness' and his 'unknowing knowing'. It is this that makes you silent, in thought as well as speech; it is this that makes your prayer so concentrated; it is this that teaches you to forsake and despise the world.

And what is more: in this you are taught to forsake and despise yourself, according to Christ's teaching in the Gospel: *Si quis vult venire post me, abneget semetipsum; tollat crucem suam et sequatur me*,[1] 'If any man will come after me,

1. Matthew 16:24.

let him forsake himself, let him bear his cross, and follow me'. In effect, in the sense we are now discussing it, he is speaking of the man who will come humbly 'not *with* me, but *after* me to the joy of heaven and to the mount of perfection'. For Christ went on ahead by nature, and we follow by grace. His nature is more important than grace, and grace is more important than *our* nature. In this way he makes us see quite clearly that we can only follow him to the mount of perfection – the purpose of contemplation – if we have first been moved to do so at the leading of grace.

And that is absolutely true. You must be quite clear – and not only you but all like you who read or hear what I am writing – that though I am saying you ought to be undertaking this work simply and boldly, yet at the same time I do not doubt for one moment that God Almighty through his grace must always be its prime instigator and sustainer, whether he makes use of any particular method or not; and that you, and your like, have but to consent and accept. The only qualification is that your consent and acceptance must be actively and readily given to this work in purity of spirit, so that it is fittingly borne up to your King. Your own spiritual insight will teach and convince you.

And since it is God who in his goodness moves and touches different souls in different ways, some with methods and some without, who is going to say that God cannot move you by this writing, or anyone else like you who hears or reads it, solely by means of me who has no worth apart from God's saving will, which is that he likes to do as he likes! I imagine it can happen. The work will be its own witness once it is put to the proof. So I beg you to prepare yourself to receive this grace from your Lord, and listen to him when he says, 'Whoever will come after me' (in the terms outlined above) 'let him forsake himself'. I ask you, how can a man better forsake himself and the world, and better despise them, than by refusing to think of any aspect of their being?

8 YOU can be quite sure of this, that though I am telling you to forget everything but the blind awareness of your naked existence, my purpose and intention all along has been that you should ultimately forget this awareness as well, in your awareness of the being of God. How this could be I set out at the beginning by showing that God is your being. But it seemed to me then that you were still in the early stages of spiritual awareness and not yet able to be raised suddenly to experience spiritually the being of God. So in order to let you mount up to this gradually I suggested that first of all you ought to get down to the naked, unseeing awareness of your own being until by persevering spiritually in this secret work you were able to rise high enough to be aware of God. For your longing and intention must always be to experience God in contemplation. And though, because of your spiritual rawness and inexperience, I tell you first of all to shroud and hide the awareness of God in the awareness of yourself, yet once you have become wiser through persevering in spiritual purity you will then strip, spoil, and divest yourself completely of any kind of self awareness in order to be clothed with the grace and awareness of God's very self.

This is what the perfect lover does: he completely strips himself of himself for the sake of the one he loves, nor will he allow himself to be clothed in anything except in that which he loves: not only for a while, but for ever to be absorbed in it, himself fully and finally forgotten. This is the work of love that none may know but the one who experiences it. This is our Lord's meaning when he says, 'Whoever will love me, let him forsake himself', as if to say 'Let him strip himself of his self if he will be truly clothed in me. I am the boundless raiment of love through all eternity and for ever.'

So whenever you look at what it is you are doing, and realize that it is yourself you are conscious of and not God, seek to be sincerely sorry, and long to be aware of God. You must want, earnestly and always, to have done with the deplorable, lamentable awareness of your own blind being, craving to escape from yourself as from poison. It is now that you forsake yourself and despise yourself most bitterly, as your Lord commands you. For it is now that you are setting your heart really seriously not on ceasing to exist (for that would be lunacy and an insult to God) but on getting rid of the conscious knowledge of your own being: this must always happen if God's love is to be experienced here below.

It is now that you realize that you cannot possibly achieve your purpose. Whatever you do, and however busy you are doing it, you always have a simple, vague awareness of your being, squeezing in between you and God – except, of course, for those occasional moments when he lets you experience himself and his abundant love.

And what is more, just as in the beginning it was your qualities that came between you and yourself, so now you reckon you have in this self of yours a heavy and painful burden indeed.

Yes. May Jesus help you now, for now you need him. All the suffering in the world outside is nothing compared with this. For now you are your own cross. And this is exactly the way to reach our Lord, who said, '"Let a man carry his cross", first in the suffering his self brings, and

then "follow me" into blessedness, to the height of perfection, to the sweet taste of my love, to the divine experience of myself.' This is where you see your need to feel
sorrow, and your desire to be rid of self-awareness. You
have to bear the burden of yourself as your cross before
you can be united to God, or experience in your spirit him
who is perfect love. It is here too, after you have been
touched and stamped by this grace, that you see something
of, and in part experience, the great value of this work,
supreme above all else.

9 TELL me, please, can anyone achieve this by intellectual means only? The answer is quite simple 'Never'.
Neither by your own native intelligence, nor by any of
your clever and ingenious meditations; not even when they
are concerned with your wretched life, or the passion of
Christ, or our Lady's joys, the saints and angels in heaven,
or again, with any faculty, skill, or characteristic of your
own or God's. Indeed, I would rather have that simple,
vague, consciousness of myself that I touched on earlier:
not of my doings, of course, but of my self. Many people
mistake what they do for what they are, but this is wrong,
for I who perform the action am one thing, and the action
I perform is another. It is the same with God: he is one
thing in himself, and his works are another. I would rather
my heart dissolved in tears because I had no awareness of
God, and was painfully burdened with my self, and so had
my longing and love kindled to experience God, than that
I should have as many ingenious, imaginative and speculative meditations as I could possibly want or discover in
books! And those, be they never so holy or pleasing to the
subtle insights of one's peculiar mind!

All the same these fine meditations are the best way for a sinner to follow when spiritually he begins to be aware of himself and of God. I would think it quite impossible – at least as I understand it, though God can do whatever he wants – for a sinner to attain such awareness without first having seen and experienced through imagination and meditation the actual deeds of himself and of God, and without grieving over what was grievous, and rejoicing over what was joyful. In fact whoever does not come this way does not really come at all, but stays outside. And this indeed is where he is, though he thinks that he is well and truly in. For many believe they are inside the spiritual door when they are still standing outside; and there they will continue to be until they seek the door in humility. Some find it quickly, and come in sooner than others. That, of course, depends on the doorkeeper, and not on the merits or gifts of the individual.

It is a wonderful household, this life of the spirit, for not only is our Lord the doorkeeper, but he is the door as well. 'Doorkeeper' he is by his Godhead: 'door' by his humanity. He says this himself in the Gospel, *Ego sum ostium. Per me si quis introierit, salvabitur; et sive egredietur sive ingredietur, pascua inveniet.*[1] *Qui vero non intrat per ostium sed ascendit aliunde, ipse fur est et latro.*[2] In the way we are interpreting it, it is as if he were saying, 'I who am almighty because of my Godhead may lawfully as doorkeeper let in whom I will, and in whatever way I like. Yet because I want there to be a universal and simple entrance, open to all who care

1. John 10:9. 'I am the door: by me if any man enter in, he shall be saved, and shall go in and out, and find pasture.' (Authorized Version).

2. John 10:1. 'He that entereth not by the door . . . but climbeth up some other way, the same is a thief and a robber.' (Authorized Version).

to come, so that none can plead that he did not know the way in, I have clothed myself in man's common humanity, and thus have made myself available. I am the door by reason of my manhood: he who enters by me will be safe.'

Those enter by the door who, when they dwell on the passion of Christ, grieve over their wickedness which caused that passion. They reprove themselves bitterly because it was they who deserved to suffer but did not, and they have pity and compassion for their good Lord who suffered so terribly and undeservedly. And then they lift up their hearts to contemplate the love and goodness of his Godhead which condescended so greatly to humble itself in our doomed human nature. These all enter by the door, and they will be saved. Whether they 'go in' contemplating his divine love and goodness, or 'out' contemplating the suffering of his manhood, they will find food for their devotions in plentiful abundance and quite sufficient to help save their souls even if they never penetrate more deeply into this life.

But he who 'enters not by the door, but climbeth up some other way' to perfection, indulging the speculative and fantastic theories of his wild, undisciplined mind, and who ignores not only the simple, open entrance mentioned above, but also the sound advice of spiritual masters, is, whoever he may be, not only a burglar of the night but a sneak thief of the day! A burglar certainly, for he goes about in the darkness of sin, banking more upon his own mental agility and purpose than on any sound advice, or the common sense way already described. And sneak thief too, for he pretends to a pure and spiritual life, by picking on the outward signs and phrases of contemplation and not its fruit. And in this way he sometimes feels within himself a longing – slight maybe – to come near to God. Bemused by this he reckons that what he is doing is good enough, when in fact it is the most dangerous thing a young man can do, to follow his eager desire without the discipline of right advice; particularly when, as in this case, he intends to climb the heights, not merely beyond his own experience, but beyond too the normal way of Christian people. That way I have already touched on, and following our Lord's teaching, I call it the door of devotion; it is the only real entrance in this life to contemplation.

10 BUT back to the matter in hand, and to what this book is about. It is of particular concern to you and others likeminded. Now if this is the door, shall the man who has found it be content merely to stand outside or on the threshold, and not come in further? I can answer for you. I say that it is always a good thing for him to wait until the great rust of his coarse, carnal nature has virtually been rubbed away – and his director and his conscience must agree that it is so. And this especially: until he knows in his inmost heart that he has been called by the personal guidance of the Spirit of God. This personal conviction is the safest and surest witness we can have in this life that the soul is being called and drawn to a more specific work of grace.

Evidence of this 'touch' can be had in this way: a man feels in his constant practice of prayer a quiet growing desire to be nearer to God; it has a special, spiritual feel about it, such as he has heard tell of, or else has found in books. If he does not feel this urge when he reads or hears about contemplation, and particularly if in his daily prayers he has no growing desire to be nearer God, let such a man stand still at the threshold, as one called to salvation but not yet to perfection.

A word of warning for you who read or listen to what I have written. It concerns this distinction I make between the man called to salvation, and the one called to perfection. When you have decided which of these is your vocation, make sure you do not go on to criticize or discuss the things that God is doing – or man, for that matter. You may not go beyond your own affairs. It is no business of yours if God calls this one to perfection, and not that; or if one responds more quickly than another. If you don't want to make mistakes, don't judge: listen for once, and take it in! If you have been called, praise God for it, and pray that you don't fall. And if you have not yet been called pray God humbly to call you when he wants. But do not teach him his business. Let him be. He has enough might, skill, and goodwill to do the best for you and for all who love him!

Whichever your role is, accept it peacefully. You have no reason to complain, for both are precious. The first is good and always essential: the second is better for him who has got it or, to put it more accurately, for him who has been taken hold of by the grace and calling of our Lord. In our pride we press on and stumble towards our goal, but in fact without him what we are doing is nothing at all, for as he himself says, *Sine mihi nihil potestis facere*,[1] which means 'Unless I first stir and prompt you, so that you have only to agree and accept it, there is nothing you can do that is perfectly pleasing to me'. And this is as it ought to be in the kind of work that this book is about.

I say all this to rebut the error and presumption of those who with their fancy 'scholarship' and 'common sense' would seek to do the work primarily themselves, God but accepting and endorsing what they do. In fact in matters

1. John 15:5. 'Without me ye can do nothing.' (Authorized Version).

contemplative it is the complete opposite. It is only here that ingenuity, learned scholarship, and natural wit have to be suppressed, in order that God may be in charge. Nevertheless in things proper to the active life a man's theological learning and natural intelligence can work in partnership with God, but only with his consent, and when too the human spirit has been checked by these three witnesses, Scripture, direction, and common sense about man's nature, stage, age, and temperament. So much is this so that a man ought not to follow the urge of his spirit, however delightful and holy it might seem – I am referring to matters of the active life – unless it agrees with his theological knowledge or his natural understanding, even when it is supported most strongly by any or all of the three witnesses I have mentioned.

It is of course demonstrably true that a man is more than just his works, and for that reason the statutes and ordinances of Holy Church will admit no man to the episcopate (the highest rank of the active life) unless the ability to fulfil that cure has been shown to be within his competence, after thorough testing. So in the active life sound theology and common sense are the chief ways of working, with God's gracious concurrence, and the approval of the three witnesses. Rightly so, for all things to do with the active life are under the control of human wisdom. But in things to do with contemplation, human wisdom, even the very greatest, has to be suppressed, so that God may be the chief worker and man but the consenter and collaborator.

So I interpret this word of the Gospel, *sine mihi nihil potestis facere* ('without me you can do nothing') in one way for actives and in another for contemplatives. For actives there must be cooperation or consent or both if anything is to be achieved, whether what is done is lawful or pleasant to a man or not. For contemplatives God must be the chief agent asking of them no more than their cooperation and consent. In general terms, then, it means that in all we do, lawful or unlawful, active or contemplative, 'without him we can do nothing'. Even in sin he is with us, but only by sufferance, not by consent, and to our final damnation, unless we humbly mend our ways. When our deeds are active and lawful he is with us by sufferance and consent, to our shame if we backslide, and to our great merit if we go forward. In contemplative matters he is with us in that he is fundamentally prompting and working in us, while we do no more than accept and consent.

All this leads on to our perfection and the spiritual union of our soul with him in perfect charity. And thus, since all people can be classified in three ways, as sinners, actives, or contemplatives, this word of our Lord may be applied to the whole world generally. He is saying 'without me' (for in the case of sinners he is present by sufferance, though not by consent; in actives he is present both by sufferance and consent; and best of all in contemplatives he is there as the chief agent and instigator) 'you can do nothing'.

There are a lot of words here, and not much relevance! All the same, I have said all this to let you know on what matters you should use your natural intelligence, and on what you should not; and how God is with you in one work, and how in another. And, perhaps, how through such knowledge you may avoid the pitfalls into which otherwise you might have stumbled had you not been warned. So now that it has been said we can leave it there, even if it has had very little to do with our subject. Now let us get on with that.

11 You may want to ask me this question, 'Could you kindly tell me by what token or tokens I can most readily and unmistakably know whether this growing desire that I feel in my prayers every day, and the attraction and pleasure I get when I read or hear of contemplation, is really a call of God to the more special work of grace, that you are writing about here? Or is it just the normal sustenance which feeds my soul, so that it stays quietly where it is, going on working with everyday grace – what you have been calling "the door" and "the normal entry" of all Christians?'

I will do my best to answer. It must be obvious to you that in this book I am setting before you two kinds of evidence by which you can check your call of God to contemplation, one within you, one outside you. Neither of these is wholly adequate, I think, without the other; but where both unite and agree together, then you have the evidence you want, complete and entire.

The first of these two ways, the interior one, is this growing desire you feel in your daily devotions. You ought to know at least this much about this desire: although in itself it is an activity of the soul, and fundamentally 'blind' – for desire is to the soul as touch, say, or walking is to the body, and both of these are 'blind'[1] physical activities as you well know – yet for all its blindness there accompanies and follows it a kind of spiritual sight, at once part cause and part means of furthering the desire. So take a good hard look at your daily spiritual exercise, what it is in itself. If it is an awareness of your own wretchedness, or the passion of Christ, or anything else to do with the early stages of our religion mentioned earlier, and if this spiritual

1. 'Blind' because they are exercised instinctively without thought. In any case they cannot see.

sight, accompanying and following your blind desire, springs from these general considerations, then it is a sure sign to me that this growing desire of yours is but the nourishing and strengthening of your spirit, to enable it to wait quietly and go on working in everyday grace; it is not a call or urge from God to grace of a more special kind.

And now the other, the second evidence, the outside one. This is the pleasant reaction you experience whenever you read about contemplation or hear it mentioned. I call this evidence 'outside' because that is where it comes from, through the windows of your physical senses, through your hearing and seeing at the time of reading. Now with regard to this second sign; if the pleasurable urge you get when contemplation is mentioned lasts with you no longer than the time you are actually reading or hearing about it, but stops at once or very soon after; and if you neither sleep with it nor find it still there when you wake up, and if it does not accompany your daily exercises, squeezing in between you and your prayers, stimulating and leading your desire on, then it is a sure sign, in my judgement, that this pleasant reaction is but the natural gladness that every Christian soul experiences when having to do with the truth, particularly when that truth is treating in depth and demonstrating clearly the characteristics that belong to perfection, of man's soul on the one hand and, more particularly, of God on the other. There is no spiritual touch of grace here, no calling of God to another more special work of grace beyond that which is at the door and threshold of Christian experience.

But if this pleasant urge you get when hearing or reading about contemplation is so overpowering that it goes to bed with you, gets up with you next morning, follows you around all day whatever you are doing, interferes with your customary daily prayers, intruding between them and you, accompanies and follows your desire, so much so that it seems to be all one desire, then even if you don't know what it is, it will affect your whole outlook and make you cheerful! While it lasts everything pleases you, and nothing upsets you. You would run a thousand miles to talk about it with someone you know has really experienced it, and yet when you get there you can find nothing to say – it does not matter who is speaking – because you want to speak of it and nothing else. Maybe your words are few, but they are significant and heartwarming: the little you utter contains a whole world of wisdom, though it can seem silly to those who depend on their natural wit. Your silence is peaceful, your talk helpful, your prayer secret, your pride proper, your behaviour humble, your laughter kind, your pleasure simple like a child at play. You love to be alone, and sit by yourself, because you suspect that people would be a hindrance, unless they were doing what you were doing. You do not care for reading or listening to books if they are not about this one thing. Then it is that both evidences, outer and inner, agree and fuse into one.

12 YES, and if both these signs and their supporting witnesses just described – assuming you have once had experience of any or all of them – were to cease for a time, and you be left high and dry, unable to experience this new fervour or to pray in your usual way, and if as a result you think you have fallen between the two, having neither and deprived of both, you are not to be too depressed over this, but accept it humbly, and patiently await the will of the Lord. For, if I can put it in picture language, you are now launched on the spiritual ocean, sailing away from

the physical state to the spiritual. Many great storms and temptations will arise at this time perhaps, and you will not know where to look for help. Everything has gone: you experience neither everyday grace nor special. Don't be unduly afraid, even if you think you have got every reason to be so. Keep loving and trusting our Lord however little you may be able to do it, for he is not far away. He will attend you, maybe very soon, and with that same grace touch you more intensely and deeply than you have ever known before. Then it is you think you are whole and have all good . . . as long as it lasts! For suddenly, almost before you are aware of it, everything has gone again, and you are abandoned in your boat, adrift and tossed about here and there, you know neither where nor whither. Yet don't despair, for I promise you he will come soon enough – indeed, whenever he likes – and will powerfully rescue you from all your troubles, far more effectively than he ever did before. Yes, and if he leaves you afterwards he will come back again. And each time, if you will but accept and humbly endure it, he will come again more wonderfully and delightfully than ever. And he will do all this because he wants you to be made as flexible to his will spiritually, as a kid-glove is to one's hand physically.

And since he sometimes comes and sometimes goes, he is testing you in two ways as he moulds you to his own pattern. By withdrawing your fervour (which means, you think, he has left you, though of course he has not) he is really testing your patience. You ought to be quite clear about this: though God does sometimes withdraw this sense of sweetness, these enthusiastic feelings, and these burning desires, he *never* on that account withdraws his grace from his chosen. Indeed, I do not believe his special grace can ever be withdrawn from his elect once they have been touched by it, but only if mortal sin should cause it.

But all this sense of sweetness, this enthusiasm, these burning desires (not in themselves grace, but only its tokens) are often taken away to test our patience; and often, too, for much other spiritual benefit, more than we can guess. For grace in itself is so pure, so spiritual, so finely spun, that it cannot be perceived by our senses. Its tokens may be, but not itself. So sometimes our Lord withholds your fervent feelings to strengthen as well as to test your patience, and not only for this reason but for many others with which I am not concerned at the moment. We must get on.

By the richness, the frequency, and the gradual development of these profound experiences I have already mentioned, with which you associate, quite wrongly, his coming, he would nourish and feed your spirit to help you persevere and to live loving and worshipping him. Thus by your patience when these experiences are absent – tokens of grace as they are – and by that vital nourishment and loving feeding of spirit when they are present, God wants to make you, joyfully and gladly, sensitive and responsive to that perfection, to spiritual union with his will. And this is what charity in all its perfection is. In this way you will be just as glad and happy not to have such feelings – if that is his will – as to have and know them without break and always.

At such time your love is chaste and perfect. It is now that you both see your God and your love, and experience him at first hand, in the very core of your being, united in spirit with him in love. You experience him as he is in himself, though blindly, as it has to be here below. Completely stripped of your self, and naked, you are clothed in him as he is in himself; you have been divested and freed from all those profound feelings that can happen in this life, be they never so sweet and holy. But in purity of spirit you perceive and feel him, rightly and perfectly –

and as he is in himself, very far removed from what we in this life fondly imagine and wrongly expect!

To your own understanding of what you feel and see this sight and experience of God as he is in himself can no more be separated from God in his own being than God himself can be separated from his own being, for he is one in essence and in nature. And just as God may not be separated from his being, because it is his nature to be united with it, so too the seeing, feeling soul cannot be separated from what it sees and feels, because it is united to it by grace. You see it is in ways like these, and by such tokens, that you get your experience and the proof (in part) of the manner and worthiness of your calling and of the urge of grace that is always going on: going on and working inwardly in your spirit, and outwardly through your reading and listening.

And if and when you and others like you have had a real experience of these signs, and have genuinely known at least one or two of them – this is enough, for very few at first are able to experience them all at once – and if you have had them thoroughly checked and tested by Scripture, director, and conscience, the time has come for you to put away intellectual exercises and clever meditations. And this remains true even when these meditations are about the Person of God or yourself, and have contributed to your understanding of it all, and have led you away from worldliness and materialism to your present state of grace. You are learning now how to bear spiritually this new understanding of yourself and God. And about this you already know much through your earlier thinking and reflection upon your doings.

Christ gave an example of this in his life. If it were true that there was no higher perfection in this life than to contemplate and love him in his humanity I believe he would not have ascended to heaven as long as this world lasted, nor have withdrawn his bodily presence from his special lovers on earth. But because there is a higher perfection which a man may reach in this life, namely, a purely spiritual experience of the love of his Godhead, he said to his disciples who were loath to let his bodily presence go – just as you are with your special meditations and intellectual subtleties! – that it was for their good that he left them physically: *Expedit vobis ut ego vadam*, 'It is for your good that I go from you physically.'[1] The Doctor[2] comments thus: 'If his human shape is not withdrawn from our sight, we shall not be able spiritually to gaze on the love of his Godhead'. So I say that it is good in due time to give up your intellectual exercises, and to learn to taste something of the love of God in your own spiritual experience.

You will come to this experience by the way I have been describing, and by God's prevenient grace. In other words you will without ceasing relax in the naked awareness of your self, ever giving your self up to God as the most precious offering you can make. But make quite sure, as I have often said, that it is *naked*, lest you be deceived. If it is to be really naked you will find it very painful at first to keep it so because, as I have said, already your intellect finds nothing to feed on. Never mind, I will love it all the better! Your faculties must lay aside for a while the natural pleasure they have in their knowledge, for as has been well said 'a man naturally wants to know'[3]. However it is quite certain one cannot taste or experience God spiritually except by grace, whatever the extent of knowledge, acquired or natural. Therefore I beg you to seek experience rather

1. John 16:7.
2. St Augustine, Sermon 143.
3. The first words of Aristotle's *Metaphysics*.

than knowledge: knowledge can often lead one astray through pride, whereas humble, loving experience does not lie. *Scientia inflat, caritas edificat.*[1] In knowledge is trouble, in experience rest.

But now you may go on to say, 'What is this rest you are speaking of? To me it seems to be all hard work, and painful at that: certainly no rest! When I set out to do what you say I find nothing but pain and battle on every side. On one hand my mind would draw me away, but I will not let it; on the other I want to be aware of God, not of myself, yet I cannot do it. There is war everywhere and pain. It is a very odd sort of rest you are speaking of!'

My answer is this, 'You are not yet used to this sort of exercise, so it is bound to be most painful for you. But once you get accustomed to it and know by experience how much profit is in it you will not willingly quit it for all the joy and rest in the world. And yet it is admittedly very painful and difficult. I still call it "rest" however, for the soul has no doubt as to what it ought to do and, what is more, it is made so much more confident (I am speaking of the time of this activity) that it is not likely to go far wrong.'

1. 1 Corinthians 8:1. 'Knowledge puffeth up, but charity edifieth.' (Authorized Version).

INTRODUCTION TO DIONYSIUS'
MYSTICAL TEACHING

Authorship

Nothing is really known, though much is conjectured, about 'Dionysius' and his *Mystica Theologia* of which the present work, under the title *Dionise Hid Divinite*, was a translation. Yet, as has been shown in the General Introduction (p. 15), the importance of this little work is out of all proportion to its size. Even today when he is universally recognized as 'pseudo', Dionysius exercises profound influence, and the current vogue for 'contemplative meditation' means that his teaching is still recognized as valid, and acceptable to twentieth-century minds. 'Pseudo' he has to be, for his writings have too many echoes of, and borrowings from, the Fathers of a much later date for him to have been a contemporary of St Paul. That he was probably a Syrian monk of the late fifth or early sixth century is as much as can be said of him.

Leading Ideas

Four books and ten letters survive bearing Dionysius' name. All are concerned to reconcile Christianity with Neoplatonism. This philosophical system was a religious updating of the teaching of Plato. Its leading exponent was Plotinus (205-70), who sought to provide a rational and satisfying basis for religious life and thought. God, he taught, is the absolutely transcendent One, and all other things are but emanations from him. Mystical experience, by which the soul has knowledge of him, can only come after a progressive shedding of all forms of human knowledge until the Absolute alone remains. 'It (God) has its centre everywhere, but its circumference nowhere.' Though

Plotinus was not a Christian, his ideas were congenial to many Christian thinkers, and Pseudo-Dionysius is one of those who have attempted to baptize him and his theology into the Church.

In *Mystica Theologia* the controlling idea is the possibility of the soul's union with God, with the consequent deification of man. This is achieved by the soul's putting aside all knowing obtained through reason and the use of the senses and by its entry into a 'cloud of unknowing'. Gradually it will be illuminated by a 'ray of divine darkness' and brought to a knowledge of God which transcends all that can be thought or said. 'We cannot apply to It either affirmation or negation, inasmuch as it transcends all affirmation by being the perfect and unique cause of all things, and transcends all negation by the pre-eminence of its simple and absolute nature.' The stages of such fulfilment are threefold, the purgative, the illuminative, and the unitive way.

The English translator claims that when the original text is difficult he has 'moche folowed the sentence of the Abbot of Seinte Victor,[1] a noble and a worthi expositour of this same book'. One such instance is in the complex opening prayer where Dionysius is obviously groping for words to express his high purpose and forgets to mention the need for loving God – if indeed he did forget it. His translator knows better: 'And for alle thees thinges ben above mynde, therfore with affecyon aboven mynde as I may, I desire to

1. He seems to have been Thomas Gallus, Abbot of St Andrew's, Vercelli (d. 1246). He was a Canon Regular of the Congregation of St Victor, and is generally known as *Vercellensis*. But the first three chapters of *Mystical Teaching* have been translated from the Latin version of Johannes Sarracenus, Vercellensis being responsible for the last two. But he wrote a Commentary on Dionysius, and this was probably used by his English translator.

purchase hem unto me with this preier.' This un-Diony-
sian but Christian emphasis on love is found elsewhere in
the book.

It is small wonder that works like *Mystical Teaching* and
The Cloud swept the theological country once they had
gained foothold. 'At deer rates,' said a medieval writer. For
now all the fundamentals of the Mystic Way have been
set out: the longing for union with God, the great effort
demanded, the threefold way, the *via negativa*, the *cloud of
unknowing*, and the indescribable realization of it all on
God's terms, and if he so wishes.

They are all there.

DIONYSIUS' MYSTICAL TEACHING

(THE TRANSLACIOUN OF DIONISE HID DIVINITE)

ST DENIS' PRAYER

You are wisdom, uncreated and eternal,
    the supreme First Cause, above all being,
    sovereign Godhead, sovereign goodness,
    watching unseen the God-inspired wisdom of Christian
      people.
Raise us, we pray, that we may totally respond
    to the supreme, unknown, ultimate, and splendid height
    of your words, mysterious and inspired.
There all God's secret matters lie covered and hidden
    under darkness both profound and brilliant, silent and
      wise.
You make what is ultimate and beyond brightness
    secretly to shine in all that is most dark.
In your way, ever unseen and intangible,
    You fill to the full with most beautiful splendour
    those souls who close their eyes that they may see.
And I, please, with love that goes on beyond mind
    to all that is beyond mind,
    seek to gain such for myself through this prayer.

PROLOGUE

THIS work is an English translation of a book St Denis wrote to Timothy, called in Latin *Mystica Theologia*. This is the book referred to in the seventieth chapter of *The Cloud of Unknowing* (written before this), where it says that Denis' writing will definitely confirm all that is written in it. So in translating it I have not only followed the strict letter of the text, but in order to explain its difficulties have made much use of the views of the Abbot of St Victor, a distinguished and worthy expositor of the same.

TIMOTHY, MY FRIEND

1 *Men can attain to this hidden deity by putting away all that is not God.*

Whenever you are prompted by grace and mean to follow up your 'blind seeing', make sure that with firm, wise, and earnest sorrow you put away your physical senses (hearing, sight, smell, taste, and touch), your spiritual senses (by which you understand things), and all that is known through these two channels. Moreover, make sure that you also put away things that are present or past and, indeed, everything that has not yet occurred, though it might well do so in the future. And as far as I can put it into intelligible words, see that you rise up with me in this grace – though we do not know how it can be – so as to be united with him who is above all being and knowledge. For it is through this passing beyond yourself and every other thing (and thereby cleansing yourself from all worldly, physical, and natural love, and from everything that can be known by the normal processes of mind) that you will be caught up in love beyond the range of intellect to the super-essential ray of divine darkness. Everything else will have gone.

Take care that none of those foolish people who live by their senses hear of these matters. 'Foolish' is my word for those who are attached to knowledge and who love things that can be known and have beginnings: they believe there is nothing supernatural beyond these. They reckon they know him 'who has made darkness his dwelling place',[1] in much the same way as they know themselves. And since,

1. Psalms 18:12.

as the prophet says, the divine teaching of these secrets is beyond them,[1] what are we to make of those even more foolish folk, who live not only by their mental powers and their own natural philosophy, but descend lower still, beneath them, and live by those bodily senses they have in common with animals? Such people do not know how to attain to the knowledge of the First Cause, who reigns supreme above all things; so they make images of the least important of visible things, and worship stocks and stones. And they say there is nothing beyond these evil figures in all their variety, which they have manufactured for themselves out of their fantastic imagination.

It may be a lot of nonsense, but that is how it is. It is up to us to see and proclaim that these 'beings' are placed in their rightful context, in him who is above knowledge and thought, in him who is the cause of them all. And, more properly and very firmly, to deny 'being' to these things in the sense we use the word of him, the sovereign Being over all, supreme in himself, and other than them all. And to hold moreover that the denial of these 'beings' does not contradict what we first said about them; rather to hold fast with the sight our faith gives to him who is above all negation of these things whether they exist actually or only potentially. For he in himself is beyond them all indeed, whether it is by negation or affirmation.

It is for this reason that godly Bartholomew, the apostle of Christ, wrote that Christ's divinity is at once vast and minute, and though the Gospel too is broad and plentiful it is, again, narrow and little. It seems to me that he was caught up to gaze on things supernatural when he said that the good cause of all can be described in many words, and also in short phrases, neither being rational nor understandable for the purpose of attaining that which is super-essen-

1. Job 28:20–21.

tially above all things that 'are'. Yet in fact he is not hidden, for he is clearly and truly accessible, admittedly not to all but only to them who pass beyond all things that exist, whether they be clean or unclean; who transcend every method, achieving whatever holy end or purpose is open to men or angels; who dispense with all divine 'lights' and heavenly sounds and works, and enter into the darkness with love; for in truth it is here, as the Bible makes clear, that he dwells who is above all.

You will see an example of this in the story which tells how the godly Moses, mildest of men, is first bidden to make himself clean, and his people too, and then to keep away from all occasion of defilement. It was after he and his people were cleansed that he heard the trumpets and the many voices, and saw shining lights which sent out vast, broad, pure, rays. After that, he had to separate himself from all his people, and with selected priests scale the topmost pinnacle of the divine ascent, the end and limit of human understanding – and to do that with all the help that grace bestows. Yet in all this he was not with God, in terms of the perfection of deity. He was contemplating an object: not God himself, who cannot be seen by human eyes. But what he saw was the place where God was. And that place symbolizes man's highest contemplation of God, for it passes beyond all human rationality and keeps it in subjection, as some mistress might do with her servants! By such contemplation the presence of him who is above all thought is shown supremely to human intelligence, setting one beyond the limits of one's natural powers. It is then that a man is released from those active powers of the soul which he can understand, and from their objectives; in other words, from the modes in which they work.

It is now that Moses with his especial love is separated from the priests already mentioned, and enters by himself into the darkness of unknowing, a darkness which is indeed hidden, one in which he forgoes all knowledge capable of being known, Always he is made to feel and experience, in a way that is invisible and intangible, the presence of him who is above all things. He has no feeling or thought of anything else at all, not even of himself. But it is as he gets away from the knowing that is always unknown that he is united to him in the best way possible, and because he knows nothing he is made to know what is beyond thought.

2 *How we are united to the Cause of all, who is above all.*

Into this supreme and dazzling darkness we pray that we may come, that by not seeing and not knowing we may see and know him who is beyond all seeing and knowing through this very act of not seeing or knowing; and at this supreme peak of being, by dismissing all things that *are*, that we may praise him who is himself above all. How to put away these things can be illustrated by the following example.

Here is a man who has a solid block of wood of immense size lying in front of him, *outside* him. *Inside* him, however, is the intention and the ability to fashion a little figure from the wood, and, correctly measured and aligned, it is in the dead centre of that block. Right away your common sense will tell you that before he can begin to see that figure clearly with his physical eyes, or show to others what now only exists within himself in his skill and vivid imagination – for the block is still intact in every part – the first requirement is that he use his skill and his tools to remove all the outer wood which cases and hides the statue from sight. In exactly the same way we have got to act with regard to this high and divine undertaking, as far as may be possible for us to understand it by so crude an example drawn from something that is basically different.

In this matter we are like a man making a picture of his simple, uncreated, 'unbegun' nature, a nature which is free both in itself and for itself; a nature found within all creatures, but not restricted to them; outside all creatures, but not excluded from them; above all creatures but not over them; beneath, but not below; behind, and not behind; before, and not before. Yet as he understands it, all the while it is joined to his mortal body he can never see it clearly, except as something covered, wrapped, and overlaid with countless things to feel, for example, and substances to understand, many and marvellous and fantastic – all conglomerated into some cumbersome garment wrapping him round like the image in the example I have just described hidden in the great, thick, solid block.

We can always get rid of this 'awkward wrapping', made up of countless pieces, without much difficulty, because the wisdom of grace in this divine work overcomes the strong opposition ranged against this mystical vision. And because wise grace puts all such away, we can cheerfully praise – and that beyond the range of the intellect – the beauty of the self in its naked, unmade, unbegun state. How? No one knows but only he who tries it, and then always and only at that very moment.

So it behoves all of us who engage in this divine work to make our negative statements in a fashion different from our positive ones. Normally our affirmations begin with those existing things that are most worthwhile, and it is later that we descend to lesser matters. But in our negative statements we begin with the least and reach up to the greatest; or alternatively we go from the highest to the lowest; or yet again, from the lowest to the highest. And then we collect them all together and put them away in order to know clearly the 'unknowing' which has nothing to do with those powers which can be known through things that exist. And we do this so that we may see that supreme essential darkness, which is shrouded in secret from all the light that comes from things that are.

3 Books of the Affirmative and Negative Ways.

It is for this reason that we have written our other theological books, particularly those which deal with positive theology, namely *The Hierarchies of Heaven*, and *The Hierarchies of the Church Militant*.[1] In both these we have demonstrated the way in which that exalted, divine, and unique nature (which is God) is one; and, also, how it is three, with the attributes which we call Fatherhood, Sonship, and Holy Spirithood; and how the lights of goodness dwelling in their heart emanate from that which is not matter, from him who alone is good in himself and through himself; and how in this dwelling in himself (in the unity of his being) and again in himself (in the Trinity of Persons) and in turn together (with mutual, eternal outpouring) they dwell unchangeably; and how the supreme, essential Jesus is made essentially and truly man. These and all such other matters dealt with in the Bible are demonstrated positively in these two books.

In the book, *The Divine Names*, it is set out clearly how God can be called 'good' or 'being' or 'life' or 'wisdom' or 'virtue' or what other attributes we can intelligently use of God. But in *The Collection of Words about God*[2] I

1. These are more generally known as *Celestial Hierarchy* and *Ecclesiastical Hierarchy*.
2. *The Symbolic Theology.*

have set out all those names that have been used of God, and drawn from the things of sense. For example, those which can be sensibly used of him, and those which are types of the divine, and those which can be used to describe his character and his beauty – and indeed those that have been used to describe his wrath and grief, his unpredictability, his inebriation, his gluttony, swearing and cursing, his sleeping and waking, and those other epithets of 'sense' that have been applied to him in some way in the Bible.

All this I imagine you have seen, and you will know how these things I speak of involve the use of many more words than do the earlier books. For it is quite plain that in the first two books of *The Hierarchies* and in the exposition of the third book of *The Divine Names* fewer words are dealt with than in this last *Collection of Words about God*. For when we are considering matters to do with the Most High the very words on which we base such consideration actually limit our understanding. So here in this present book when we are entering the darkness that is beyond mind, not only do we find that words are inadequate, but everything we say seems fantastic and utterly irrational. In all the other books our description has come down from the highest things to the lowest, and when it has descended a long way it has spread out to a multitude of things. But now in this present work we are progressing from the lowest things to the highest, and after we have ascended some way – and sometimes it comes sooner than at others – it can become very restricting. And always when the ascent is complete there will be nothing one can say of it, for it is wholly united to that which is beyond all speech.

But perhaps you are going to ask, 'Why is it that in affirmative theology we begin with those things that are most worthy, but in negative theology with those that are least?' The reason is this: when we would describe God by stating all the things we can understand of him – him who in himself is above all affirmation and understanding – it is most suitable that we first of all state those matters which are most worthy and close to him. If on the other hand we want to describe him by eliminating all understandable things, it is most suitable that we first dismiss all things that are most unlike him. For example, more akin and like to him are 'life' and 'goodness' than, say, 'air' or 'stone'. By the same token one would be more likely to ascribe to him 'speech' and 'understanding' than 'gluttony' and 'lunacy'. Yet in himself he is above all that can be said or understood of him.

4 *God who is the cause of them all is none of the things we can know by our senses.*

So first of all we remove from God everything that has no substance, and everything that has no existence, beginning with the most remote; for such a 'thing' is more remote than those things which exist but do not live. And then we take away these existing but not living things, for they are further off than something that exists and lives. After that we eliminate the existing, living things which have no feeling, for they are further off than those that can feel. Next go feeling things that have no reason or understanding, for they are more remote than those which possess both. And together with all these we remove from God everything physical, and all that has to do with bodily matters like shape, form, quality, size, weight, position, visibility, sensitivity, action, and suffering; the disorderly, fleshly greed; the complications of material passions; the weakness controlled by haphazard senses; the necessity of light; all breeding and corrupting and dividing and suffering; and all the passing moments of time. For he is none of these things, nor has he any of these things, nor any other thing that we know by our senses.

5 *God who is the cause of them all is none of the things we can understand.*

And so we who have begun our denials and removals by reaching the 'highest' of the things we can understand say that God is neither soul nor angel; he has no imagination or opinion or reason or understanding; nor is he reason or understanding; nor can he be described or understood. Moreover, and here we are moving from high things to low, he has no number, order, greatness, smallness, equality, likeness, unlikeness; he neither stands still nor moves, keeps silence nor speaks. And if we turn back to the highest matters to end our denyings there, we assert that he has no virtue, nor is he virtue or light; he is not life or substance or age or time; we can understand nothing about him, nor is he knowledge or truth or kingdom or wisdom or singularity or unity or Godhead or goodness. Nor in the sense that we understand 'spirit' is he spirit; there is no sonship or fatherhood, nor anything else that is known by us or by anyone else. He is none of the things that have no being, none of the things that have being. None of the things that are known know him for what he is. Nor does he know the things that exist for what they are in themselves, but only for what they are in him. Nor is there any way by which we can reach him through reason or understanding: he has no name; we cannot know him; he is neither darkness nor light, error nor truth. Speaking generally there is no affirmation we can make of him, nothing we can deny of him. When we attribute something to him, or deny any or all of the things which he is not, we do not describe him or abolish him, nor in any way that we can understand do we affirm him or deny him. For the perfect and unique cause of all is of necessity beyond compare with the highest of all imaginable heights, whether by affirmation or denial. And this surpassing non-understandability is 'un-understandably' above every affirmation and denial.

INTRODUCTION TO THE EPISTLE OF PRAYER

Leading Ideas

This little tract is a gem; perhaps indeed one of 'purest ray serene' that has lain too long in 'the dark unfathom'd caves of ocean' and is due now for salvage. Certainly in the original it is a beautiful piece of writing, balanced, rich, and complex, with all the subtle literary characteristics we associate with the author of *The Cloud*. It is written for a young contemplative who has asked 'how to reule his hert in tyme of his preier'. The treatment remains, after six centuries, remarkably fresh and skilful.

Good praying, says the author, has two ingredients: fear of God, and hope in him, a hope which at once leads on to love. He suggests that the young disciple should accept as a possibility that he might die before his prayer is ended – an idea as valid in these thrombotic days as when it was first made. Though almost certainly he will survive, it will, in the words of Dr Johnson's famous aphorism, 'concentrate his mind wonderfully'. But this proper fear will lead on to hope in the grace of God to pardon and help.

He uses a favourite figure of the Middle Ages to illustrate the developing experience of prayer, that of a tree full of fruit. The tree's root is *dread* of God, its trunk *hope*, the branches *love*, and the fruit *reverent affection*. This last, as long as it is attached to the tree, partakes of its nature, but once it has been picked and is independent of it (that is, of fear and hope) it gains a new scent and sweetness, and is 'food fit for a king'. It is now, the illustration is telling us, that the contemplative loves God perfectly, for himself alone and not for any fringe benefits. This is 'chaste love', a phrase synonymous with other key expressions, 'fruit of the tree', 'perfect prayer', 'perfection of virtues', 'mystical theology', the soul's marriage to God, and so on. The acquisition of this perfect love is, however, no easy matter. Together with the traditional disciplines imposed by the laws of Holy Church (and as in all these writings, sacramental confession in particular) the 'swete kirnel' can only be eaten 'bot if thou crakke first the harde schelle, and bite of the bitter bark'.

THE EPISTLE OF
PRAYER

(A PISTLE OF PREIER)

i You have asked me how to control your mind when you are saying your prayers, and I will do my best to answer.

ii What I would say is this: I think what is going to help you most when you start your prayer – and it doesn't matter whether it is long or short or what – is to make quite sure that you are certain that you will die by the time it is ended, that you will finish before your prayer does! Now don't go thinking that I am asking anything crazy! Why? There is not a man alive today who would dare deny its possibility, to say you would necessarily live longer than your prayer. So it is quite in order for you to think this way.

iii I suggest you do this, for if you do you will see that with your general awareness of your own wretchedness, and with this particular sense of the short time left you for amendment, it will bring to your heart a genuine feeling of dread. And this feeling you will have deep down inside you, unless, which God forbid, you flatter and deceive your unreal, unspiritual, unseeing heart with deceitful lies and pretended promises of longer life. Almost certainly you will live longer than your prayer, but it is always wrong to bank on it, and a mistake to promise it to yourself. The fact is that this depends solely on God, and all you can do is to wait blindly on his will; you cannot even be sure of a moment of life – and a moment is as short as, or less than, the twinkling of an eye. So if you are to pray wisely (as the prophet bids when he says *Psallite sapienter*[1]) see that at the outset you get this real sense of dread. For

1. Psalms 47:7.

the same prophet says in another psalm, *Initium sapientiae est timor Domini*.[1] The beginning of wisdom is the fear of the Lord God.

iv But dread is no good as a foundation for anything unless it is for even more dread, the kind that sinks down into deep depression. So you must link your original idea with this further thought: you are to believe that if through the grace of God you can clearly speak the words of your prayer and bring it to its conclusion, or if you do die before you reach the end having done what you could, then God will accept it as full payment for all your neglect from the time your life began up to that very moment. Naturally I am assuming that before this you have deliberately, conscientiously, and lawfully amended your life according to the rules of Holy Church about confession. This little prayer, however short, will be accepted by God for your total salvation should you die, and for even greater perfection if you go on living. This is the goodness of God which, as the prophet says, will forsake no one who truly trusts him, and who intends to mend his ways.[2]

v Amendment depends on two things: departing from evil, and doing good. There are no quicker ways of achieving these than those two thoughts already mentioned. For what can better take away the love of sinning from one's life than a real fear of death? And what moves one to live more fervently and to do good more than confident hope in the mercy and goodness of God, brought about by this second thought? The reason is that when these two are combined they provide a sure staff of hope to hold on to in all your good works.

vi With the aid of this staff you may safely climb the high peak of perfection, the perfect love of God, though

1. Psalms 111:10.
2. Psalms 37 passim.

to begin with it is imperfect, as you will be learning later. For with your general understanding and personal experience of God's mercy and goodness – he accepted your paltry little service as full payment for your long neglect – you cannot but feel a great surge of love for him who has been so merciful and good to you. And if you have done it according to what I have told you, you will have been helped on your way in prayer by your staff, Hope. The spiritual proof of this exercise is found in the reverent love a man has for God in his time of prayer. It is caused by this basic dread and this stirring of love. For reverence is nothing but dread and love blended together by the staff of a sure hope. I think the fact of our devotion proves that it works, for devotion, as St Thomas the divine doctor says, is only the readiness and the will of a man to do the things that belong to the service of God.[1] Everyone can prove it for himself, for he who does God's service in this matter knows how ready his will is for it. I think St Bernard agrees with this when he says that everything should be done swiftly and gladly;[2] swiftly, because we fear: gladly, because we love and hope and trust in his mercy.

vii   Moreover I am sure I would rather have his reward who continues in such work (even if he never does penance beyond that enjoined by Holy Church) than I would have the collective reward of all those who have done penance from the beginning of creation until now – who have done their penance but not this work. I am not saying that the bare thought itself of these two things is profitable, but that the reverent love, brought about more by these two thoughts than by anything else, is the thing that counts. And this is the only thing that matters, this alone and nothing else whatever, whether it is fastings, vigils, hairshirts,

1. *Summa Theologica* II, ii, 82.
2. *Vitis Mystica* XIX.

or what. This is what pleases Almighty God, and merits his reward. No soul can be rewarded without it. After all, the extent to which it is done will govern the extent of its reward. Who does much of the one will have much of the other; who does less will receive less. These other things (fastings, vigils, hairshirts, and such like) are useful only insofar as they help towards this end. Without this they are nothing, but this without them can sometimes be sufficient and complete in itself. Often people achieve it effectively without any such aids. I say all this so that with this knowledge you can value and commend each thing as it is, more the more, less the less. Often ignorance is the cause of much error. Often, too, it is through ignorance that physical practices (fasting and so on) are valued and commended more highly than the spiritual works of virtue or the reverent love I have been speaking about. Therefore I am going to add a little more to what I have already said about the reward and worthwhileness of this reverent love. And as a result you will be better instructed in this exercise than has been the case so far.

viii   All this business of reverent dread which I spoke of earlier, when it has been caused by these two thoughts of dread and hope, can well be likened to a tree full of fruit. Of this tree *dread* is the part that is in the earth, the root, and *hope* is the part above, the trunk and the branches. When hope is steadfast and sure it is the trunk: when it moves men to deeds of love, it is the branches. But always the fruit is this reverent affection. Too, as long as the fruit is attached to the tree it always shares in the fresh smell of the tree. But after a while, when it has been picked and is fully ripe, it loses its tree smell, and is food fit for a king. Before, it was food for slaves. It is in this time that this reverent affection is such a help, as has been said. So get ready to pick this fruit from its tree and to offer it up to the King of Heaven on high. Then you will be called God's own child, who loves him with a pure love, for his own sake, and not for what he gives.

ix What I mean is this: Almighty God in his goodness has shown innumerable kindnesses to every living soul. And they are more than enough to cause us to love him with all our heart and mind and strength. Yet were it possible, however unlikely, for a soul to be as fine and strong and clever as all the saints and angels put together, but never to have had opportunity to appreciate the worthiness of God or his kindness, such a soul when he saw the love of God as it is in himself and in all its abundance, would be ravished out of himself to love God until his heart would burst, so lovely, so attractive, so good, and so splendid is he.

x How wonderful and glorious it is to speak of the love of God! No man can express it precisely, nor indeed can he really understand the least thing about it except by using impossible illustrations beyond his comprehension! And this is what I mean when I talk of 'loving him with a pure love, for his own sake, and not for what he gives'. I am not saying – though I could well do so – that we are not to love him much because of his gifts, but rather that we should love him infinitely more for his own sake. What I am meaning when I talk about perfection and the reward of this reverent affection can be expressed in a more lofty way: a perfect soul, whose affection has been touched by the conscious presence of God as he is in himself, and whose reason has been enlightened by the clear beam of eternal light (which is God) so that he sees and feels the loveliness of God in himself, at that moment loses all recollection of any good or kind thing that God has ever done for him. What previously caused him to love God he now neither feels nor sees, for he has God himself.

xi So although in speaking of perfection in general it could be said that the great goodness and kindness that God shows us in this life are sufficient and exalted reasons for loving God, yet, since we are concerned with the aim and attainment of perfection (which is the underlying purpose of my writing), a perfect lover of God, fearful of hindering perfection, at this time seeks as the end of his perfection no other cause for loving God than God himself. Which is what I mean when I say that chaste love is to love God for himself and not for what he gives.

xii So, to stick to my illustration, prepare to pick the fruit from the tree, and to offer it up to the King of Heaven by itself, so that your love may be pure. For all the time you offer him the unripe fruit which is still on the tree you are like an unchaste woman who loves a man more for what he gives than for what he is. And the reason I am saying this is because it seems to me that your dread of dying, and the shortness of time left you, and your hope that your negligence may be forgiven, is what makes you as reverent in the service of God as you are. If this is so, then your fruit still has on it the smell of the tree. And though it pleases God in a way, it does not please him altogether, because your love is not pure. Love is pure when you ask God neither for release from suffering, nor for increase of joy, nor for the sweetness of his love here below – except when you need sweetness to freshen up your spiritual forces lest they should fail – but when you ask from God only himself. Then you neither care nor consider whether you are in pain or bliss, so long as you have him whom you love. This is pure love; this is perfect love. So get ready to separate the fruit from the tree; in other words, your reverent affection from your earlier thoughts of dread and hope. Then you can offer it to God by itself, ripe and pure, not caused by anything beneath him, or by something in which he has a share (yes, even when it is chief) but caused only by himself.

xiii   And then it is as rewarding as I am saying it is. For it is plainly and indubitably held by all who are skilled in spiritual knowledge and in the love of God that as often as a man's love for God is kindled without anything in particular to prompt it (without, that is, any special reminder or thought to cause it to rise up) just so often does it deserve eternal life. And because a soul thus disposed (that is to say, who is offering up the fruit ripe and separated from its tree) may without means be raised to God times without number in the course of a single hour, so beyond my power to describe does it deserve, I say, through the grace of God, who is the chief agent, to be raised up to joy. So be ready to offer him the fruit, ripe and picked from the tree.

xiv   Nevertheless, the fruit which is upon the tree and is continually offered as far as human frailty will permit, deserves salvation too. But the fruit, ripe and separate, instinctively offered to God without prompting – that is perfection! You can see in this way that the tree is good, although I am suggesting that you pick the fruit off it for greater perfection. This is why I plant it in your garden: I want you to gather its fruit and keep it for your Lord, and I want you to know how it works in uniting man's soul to God, making it one with him in love and will.

xv   As St Paul says, *Qui adhaeret Deo, unus spiritus est cum illo*,[1] 'Who draws near to God' as we do through this reverent affection, 'is one spirit with God.' Although God and we are two, and distinct by nature, yet by grace we are so joined together that we become but one spirit. And this is because there is unity of love and agreement of will. And in this unity is made the marriage between God and

1. 1 Corinthians 6:17.

the soul; and it is indissoluble (though the fervour and the heat of this experience may cease for a time) unless broken by mortal sin. When it is spiritually experiencing this unity a loving soul may say (and sing if it so desires) that holy word in the Bible's Song of Songs, *Dilectus meus mihi et ego illi*,[1] 'My Beloved is mine and I am his'. By which it is understood 'that you will be united and spiritually secured by grace on his part, and by a loving consent and glad spirit on yours'.

xvi   Therefore climb up by this tree, as I said at the beginning, and when you get to the fruit (that reverent affection which will always be with you), and you think over those two thoughts we have spoken of, not deceiving yourself with lies (as I have also said), then you will take great care of the work going on in your soul at such time. You will prepare yourself as best you can through grace to be humbled before God's sublimity, so that you may accustom yourself to this work should it come at some other time unprompted by any thought. Surely this is what is so rewarding, as I have suggested. The further its separation from the tree, from any thought, and the more often it happens, suddenly, delightfully, unexpectedly, without prompting, the sweeter is its scent, and the more pleasing to heaven's exalted King. And whenever you feel sweetness and comfort in what you are doing, then he is breaking open the fruit and giving you part of your own present.

xvii   What you feel in your heart to be so hard and such a strain, with no initial comfort, is due to the greenness of the fruit still on the tree, or of the fruit just picked: it sets your teeth on edge! Yet it is essential to you. There is no reason why you should eat the sweet kernel without having first to crack its hard shell or bite its bitter bark. But if your teeth are weak, in other words, your spiritual strength, then

1. Canticle 2:16.

I advise you to apply some stratagem, for 'skill is better than brute force'.

xviii There is another reason why I set this tree in your garden for you to climb up. God can do what he wants, of course, yet as I understand it, it is not possible for a man to attain perfection in this work unless these two means, or two others like them, come first. And yet the perfection of this work is its suddenness, without means. So I reckon these are yours; not your own property – that would be sin – but yours given by God's grace, and through me, his unworthy messenger. For be sure of this: each thought that prompts you to be good, whether it comes from within by angel-messenger, or from outside by a human one, is but an instrument of grace, given, sent, and chosen by God himself to work within your soul.

xix And this is the reason why I advise you to take these two before all others. For just as a man is a blend of two substances, physical and spiritual, so it is necessary to have two distinct means by which to reach perfection (both these substances will be united and immortal at the resurrection on the Last Day) so that either substance can be raised to perfection in this life by what is common to both: 'dread' for the physical substance, and 'hope' for the spiritual. I think this is both right and proper. For as nothing transports the body from all affection for earthly things sooner than a conscious dread of death, so there is nothing that sooner or more fervently raises the affection of a sinful soul to the love of God than the certain hope of forgiveness for all his sins. So I command you to climb up by these two thoughts.

xx But if so be that your good angel – or some man perhaps – teaches you inwardly in your spiritual understanding that there are two other means that you think are more suitable to your disposition, then you may take them, and safely leave these without blame. All the same as far as I understand it at the present I think that these two will be a real help to you, and not too unsuited to your make-up. I feel this to be true for you. So if you think they do you good, give God sincere thanks. And for the love of God pray for me. Do it because I am such a wretch, and you do not know how it goes with me. No more at present, but God's blessing and mine be with you. Read it often, and don't forget it. Really try it out, and fly from everything that hinders you, and all occasions of hindrance, in the Name of Jesus. Amen.

FOR THE BEST IN PAPERBACKS, LOOK FOR THE

In every corner of the world, on every subject under the sun, Penguin represents quality and variety – the very best in publishing today.

For complete information about books available from Penguin – including Pelicans, Puffins, Peregrines and Penguin Classics – and how to order·them, write to us at the appropriate address below. Please note that for copyright reasons the selection of books varies from country to country.

In the United Kingdom: For a complete list of books available from Penguin in the U.K., please write to *Dept E.P., Penguin Books Ltd, Harmondsworth, Middlesex, UB7 0DA*

In the United States: For a complete list of books available from Penguin in the U.S., please write to *Dept BA, Penguin, 299 Murray Hill Parkway, East Rutherford, New Jersey 07073*

In Canada: For a complete list of books available from Penguin in Canada, please write to *Penguin Books Canada Ltd, 2801 John Street, Markham, Ontario L3R 1B4*

In Australia: For a complete list of books available from Penguin in Australia, please write to the *Marketing Department, Penguin Books Australia Ltd, P.O. Box 257, Ringwood, Victoria 3134*

In New Zealand: For a complete list of books available from Penguin in New Zealand, please write to the *Marketing Department, Penguin Books (NZ) Ltd, Private Bag, Takapuna, Auckland 9*

In India: For a complete list of books available from Penguin, please write to *Penguin Overseas Ltd, 706 Eros Apartments, 56 Nehru Place, New Delhi, 110019*

In Holland: For a complete list of books available from Penguin in Holland, please write to *Penguin Books Nederland B. V., Postbus 195, NL–1380AD Weesp, Netherlands*

In Germany: For a complete list of books available from Penguin, please write to *Penguin Books Ltd, Friedrichstrasse 10 – 12, D–6000 Frankfurt Main 1, Federal Republic of Germany*

In Spain: For a complete list of books available from Penguin in Spain, please write to *Longman Penguin España, Calle San Nicolas 15, E–28013 Madrid, Spain*

Netochka Nezvanova Fyodor Dostoyevsky

Dostoyevsky's first book tells the story of 'Nameless Nobody' and introduces many of the themes and issues which will dominate his great masterpieces.

Selections from the Carmina Burana A verse translation by David Parlett

The famous songs from the *Carmina Burana* (made into an oratorio by Carl Orff) tell of lecherous monks and corrupt clerics, drinkers and gamblers, and the fleeting pleasures of youth.

Fear and Trembling Søren Kierkegaard

A profound meditation on the nature of faith and submission to God's will which examines with startling originality the story of Abraham and Isaac.

Selected Prose Charles Lamb

Lamb's famous essays (under the strange pseudonym of Elia) on anything and everything have long been celebrated for their apparently innocent charm; this major new edition allows readers to discover the darker and more interesting aspects of Lamb.

The Picture of Dorian Gray Oscar Wilde

Wilde's superb and macabre novella, one of his supreme works, is reprinted here with a masterly Introduction and valuable Notes by Peter Ackroyd.

A Treatise of Human Nature David Hume

A universally acknowledged masterpiece by 'the greatest of all British Philosophers' – A. J. Ayer

A Passage to India   E. M. Forster

Centred on the unresolved mystery in the Marabar Caves, Forster's great work provides the definitive evocation of the British Raj.

The Republic   Plato

The best-known of Plato's dialogues, *The Republic* is also one of the supreme masterpieces of Western philosophy whose influence cannot be overestimated.

The Life of Johnson   James Boswell

Perhaps the finest 'life' ever written, Boswell's *Johnson* captures for all time one of the most colourful and talented figures in English literary history.

Remembrance of Things Past (3 volumes)   Marcel Proust

This revised version by Terence Kilmartin of C. K. Scott Moncrieff's original translation has been universally acclaimed – available for the first time in paperback.

Metamorphoses   Ovid

A golden treasury of myths and legends which has proved a major influence on Western literature.

A Nietzsche Reader   Friedrich Nietzsche

A superb selection from all the major works of one of the greatest thinkers and writers in world literature, translated into clear, modern English.

Aeschylus	**The Oresteia**
	(Agamemnon/Choephori/Eumenides)
	Prometheus Bound/The Suppliants/Seven
	Against Thebes/The Persians
Aesop	**Fables**
Apollonius of Rhodes	**The Voyage of Argo**
Apuleius	**The Golden Ass**
Aristophanes	**The Knights/Peace/The Birds/The Assembly**
	Women/Wealth
	Lysistrata/The Acharnians/The Clouds
	The Wasps/The Poet and the Women/The Frogs
Aristotle	**The Athenian Constitution**
	The Ethics
	The Politics
Aristotle/Horace/	
Longinus	**Classical Literary Criticism**
Arrian	**The Campaigns of Alexander**
Saint Augustine	**City of God**
	Confessions
Boethius	**The Consolation of Philosophy**
Caesar	**The Civil War**
	The Conquest of Gaul
Catullus	**Poems**
Cicero	**The Murder Trials**
	The Nature of the Gods
	On the Good Life
	Selected Letters
	Selected Political Speeches
	Selected Works
Euripides	**Alcestis/Iphigenia in Tauris/Hippolytus/The**
	Bacchae/Ion/The Women of Troy/Helen
	Medea/Hecabe/Electra/Heracles
	Orestes/The Children of Heracles/
	Andromache/The Suppliant Woman/
	The Phoenician Women/Iphigenia in Aulis

PENGUIN CLASSICS

Pliny	**The Letters of the Younger Pliny**
Plutarch	**The Age of Alexander** (Nine Greek Lives)
	The Fall of the Roman Republic (Six Lives)
	The Makers of Rome (Nine Lives)
	The Rise and Fall of Athens (Nine Greek Lives)
Polybius	**The Rise of the Roman Empire**
Procopius	**The Secret History**
Propertius	**The Poems**
Quintus Curtius Rufus	**The History of Alexander**
Sallust	**The Jugurthine War** and **The Conspiracy of Cataline**
Seneca	**Four Tragedies** and **Octavia**
	Letters from a Stoic
Sophocles	**Electra/Women of Trachis/Philoctetes/Ajax**
	The Theban Plays (King Oedipus/Oedipus at Colonus/Antigone)
Suetonius	**The Twelve Caesars**
Tacitus	**The Agricola** and **The Germania**
	The Annals of Imperial Rome
	The Histories
Terence	**The Comedies (The Girl from Andros/The Self-Tormentor/The Eunuch/Phormio/The Mother-in-Law/The Brothers)**
Thucydides	**The History of the Peloponnesian War**
Tibullus	**The Poems** and **The Tibullan Collection**
Virgil	**The Aeneid**
	The Eclogues
	The Georgics
Xenophon	**A History of My Times**
	The Persian Expedition

PENGUIN CLASSICS

PENGUIN CLASSICS

Saint Anselm	**The Prayers and Meditations**
Saint Augustine	**The Confessions**
Bede	**A History of the English Church and People**
Chaucer	**The Canterbury Tales**
	Love Visions
	Troilus and Criseyde
Froissart	**The Chronicles**
Geoffrey of Monmouth	**The History of the Kings of Britain**
Gerald of Wales	**History and Topography of Ireland**
	The Journey through Wales and The Description of Wales
Gregory of Tours	**The History of the Franks**
Julian of Norwich	**Revelations of Divine Love**
William Langland	**Piers the Ploughman**
Sir John Mandeville	**The Travels of Sir John Mandeville**
Marguerite de Navarre	**The Heptameron**
Christine de Pisan	**The Treasure of the City of Ladies**
Marco Polo	**The Travels**
Richard Rolle	**The Fire of Love**
Thomas à Kempis	**The Imitation of Christ**

ANTHOLOGIES AND ANONYMOUS WORKS

The Age of Bede
Alfred the Great
Beowulf
A Celtic Miscellany
The Cloud of Unknowing and Other Works
The Death of King Arthur
The Earliest English Poems
Early Christian Writings
Early Irish Myths and Sagas
Egil's Saga
The Letters of Abelard and Heloise
Medieval English Verse
Njal's Saga
Seven Viking Romances
Sir Gawain and the Green Knight
The Song of Roland